SHARK FISHING

BY
CAPT. MIKE SCHMIDT

Bloomington, IN Milton Keynes, UK

AuthorHouse™
1663 Liberty Drive, Suite 200
Bloomington, IN 47403
www.authorhouse.com
Phone: 1-800-839-8640

AuthorHouse™ UK Ltd.
500 Avebury Boulevard
Central Milton Keynes, MK9 2BE
www.authorhouse.co.uk
Phone: 08001974150

© 2004, 2005, 2006, 2007 Capt. Mike Schmidt. All rights reserved.

No part of this book may be reproduced, stored in a retrieval system, or transmitted by any means without the written permission of the author.

First published by AuthorHouse 3/6/2007

ISBN: 1-4259-1874-3 (sc)

First Edition
Printed in the United States of America
Bloomington, Indiana

This book is printed on acid-free paper.
Front Cover design by Jason Calogeros, photo by Capt. Mike Schmidt
Additional Design and Layout by Mark Unger, Buffalo, NY

Capt. Mike Schmidt and Chum Line Productions
Call 1-800-766-3425 Ext: 1002

Website www.Sharks.us

Email Chum@Sharks.us

For a big game shark fishing adventures go to http://www.Sharks.us/charter/
Or call Capt. Mike Schmidt at 1-800-766-3425 Cell 1-818-262-6022

Acknowledgements

To my family, whose encouragement and inspiration brought this book into being. To my close friend, John Mazur, for always standing by my side.

Contents

Introduction	Page vii
The Mako Shark	Page 1
Safety Equipment for Boat & Passenger Safety	Page 16
Finding Shark Grounds	Page 28
Equipment	Page 44
Gaffs	Page 46
Knives	Page 52
Rods & Reels	Page 62
Belts & Harnesses	Page 76
Boat Tools and Fishing Equipment	Page 79
Electronic Attracting Device	Page 84
Line, Hooks & Rigging Leaders	Page 86
Chum, Chum Mashers, and Chum Systems	Page 101
Barrel System	Page 113
Pre-Slicking and Power Chumming	Page 119
Tying Line & Hooks	Page 123
Rigging Bait	Page 127
Trolling and Downrigger Fishing	Page 139
Setting up the Spread	Page 141
Hooking & Fighting Sharks; Boating the Mako	Page 146
Tagging and Releasing Sharks	Page 164
Butchering the Mako	Page 171
Cooking the Shark	Page 179
Shark Jaws	Page 183
Tournaments	Page 191
Laws	Page 200
Shark Stories	Page 202
Appendix	Page 229
About the Author	Page 237

Introduction

Take a journey of imagination on an African Safari; you are pursuing one of the most dangerous creatures on earth, the African lion. Your heart pounds as that vicious, ruthless beast stares you straight in the eye. Meeting his unwavering gaze with your own determined glare, you whip out your weapon and take the ferocious monster down. You can't hunt lions anymore, but you can still experience the adrenaline rush of squaring off with a predatory brute. Shark fishing, the last frontier for the truly wild animal hunt, can provide the thrill of your life.

Watch your favorite action film's most electrifying scene, and imagine being a part of the action. You might be a dragon-slayer, a lone warrior questing to unfamiliar territory to challenge the ruthless behemoth that reigns over an entire city. With a sturdy shield, a faithful sword and a trusty steed, you venture forth to conquer the beast.

Shark fishing electrifies you in the same way. Your boat is your chariot, your motors are your steeds, your gaff is your sword, and your rod is your shield. The "dragon" is a 1,000 pound gargantuan shark with guillotine jaws. Lured from the depths of the sea and tricked into biting your hook, this unpredictable opponent duels with incredible power. You're on his turf, and he's pretty confident you don't stand a chance. In a brain versus brawn battle, you engage a creature from the top of the food chain, whose speed and power rules the sea.

No one knows everything there is to know about shark fishing, but as one who challenges these monsters and wins, I can offer you some valuable advice. This book is designed to help you understand the sport of shark fishing, improve your catches and possibly even save your life. Though it is my personal passion to catch these leviathans of the ocean, I have a huge amount of respect for them. Shark fishing is about the excitement of the entire experience, not just catching trophies and dinner. I release most of my catches. Always remember while you're in the water that the ecosystem is a very delicate environment and it should be treated with care and respect. Please fish responsibly.

Almost every tool used in the sport is sharp: hooks, gaffs, tag poles, knives, bait needles and more. Sharks have extremely sharp teeth and immense strength. Add a rocking boat to the equation and the chance of an accident is likely every time you go out to sea.

In the United States, fishing is the number one sport with the largest number of participants; it also has the most injuries and accidents. Because of this, safety is always my number one concern; this book is infused with safety tips.

Helpful and necessary equipment is listed throughout this book. I do not endorse any of these products, make no guarantee of how they will perform for you, and am not liable for any damage you receive while using them. I am not responsible for any injuries caused by sharks or fishing for sharks. Reading this book doesn't ensure protection against injury or harm.

In my 25 years of shark fishing, I've perfected my techniques and gear. After trying numerous other methods, reading countless books and magazines, watching videos, attending seminars, and tweaking my gear, I've figured out what works and what doesn't. Coupled with my own tactics and experience, I've come up with a near-perfect system. This book will teach you techniques that utilize the latest technologies, such as internet, satellites, weather maps, thermal equipment, electronics, and electronic attractant devices, plus safety equipment that are better than ever before. It will show you how to read the sky and water utilizing this new technology. In the last seven tournaments I fished, I placed seven times using the techniques shown in this book.

Anyone can take a bucket of bloody chum, throw it in the water, and hope for Jaws to swim up to the boat. It's not likely, but if it does happen, the odds are that you and your equipment won't be ready. This book is based on 25 years of solid experience; take my success and my trials and errors into consideration and you will definitely be better prepared for big game shark fishing.

Good luck and happy hunting,
Capt. Mike Schmidt

The Mako Shark

In sports, which has a greater draw -- professional sports or amateur sports? Which is more captivating, big leagues or minor leagues? In this competitive world, you're always drawn to the best of the best. When it comes to fishing for sharks, Makos are the best.

Mako sharks are very fast fish. They are quick thinkers and quick to adapt to their environment and circumstances. They demonstrate an attitude. They are at the top of the food chain, an apex predator. Their warm-blooded bodies (unlike other species of sharks) turn them into the ferocious hunters, worthy opponents for any man.

Makos are not your typical sharks. Just looking for Makos is a superior challenge, they can be very hard to find. You have to *hunt* them by finding their feeding areas. You have to think like a Mako to find a Mako, which makes the hunt challenging.

Once you do find Makos, things get interesting. Your quarry may size you up, recognize the danger of the situation and not get tricked into biting your hook. When you do manage to hook one, he may turn on you, charge your boat, and take a few bites out of the hull. Once hooked, unlike other sharks, Makos will come after their tormenters instead of just trying to get away.

Makos seem to possess an intellect that is greater than other sharks and big game fish. When you fight a Mako, you can see it pause to think, examine the area, and plan its next move. This results in spectacular battles!

Blue sharks are known as blue dogs and thresher sharks are known as bulls of the sea. Makos are living, breathing, sea monsters, with the intelligence and tenacity to enforce their own will. They are worthy opponents for any sport fisherman.

The Mako Shark

The Mako shark is one of the oldest creatures in the sea, predating the dinosaurs. The Shortfin Mako (Isurus oxyrinchus) has prowled the oceans for millions of years.

Makos are often called the mackerel or bonito shark. The largest Mako caught off the U.S. West Coast was 351 cm (11.5 feet). The typical size of west coast Makos ranges from 213-244 cm (6-7 ft) but they can reach a size of up to 364 cm (143 inches).

The streamlined body of the Mako shark makes it a very graceful and speedy shark. Makos are the fastest sharks, capable of attaining speeds of up to 60 miles per hour. The Mako holds the speed record for long distance travel, approximately 2130 km (1320 miles) in 37 days, and an average of about 58 km (36 miles) per day.

The Mako's luminous, metallic-cobalt color and their pointed snout are distinctive features. Their swimming pattern is also unique. Unlike other sharks, the Mako is warm-blooded, which allows for heat retention from muscular activity. Being warm-blooded allows the Mako to utilize their muscle mass more efficiently, resulting in faster swimming speeds.

Mako sharks are able to maintain body temperatures greater than that of the water in which they swim. In order to maintain a warm body in cold water, Makos assert a high level of activity and ingest large quantities of food. It's common to land Makos with huge masses of food (sea lions, dolphins, or tuna) in their stomach; yet they still pursue an angler's small mackerel.

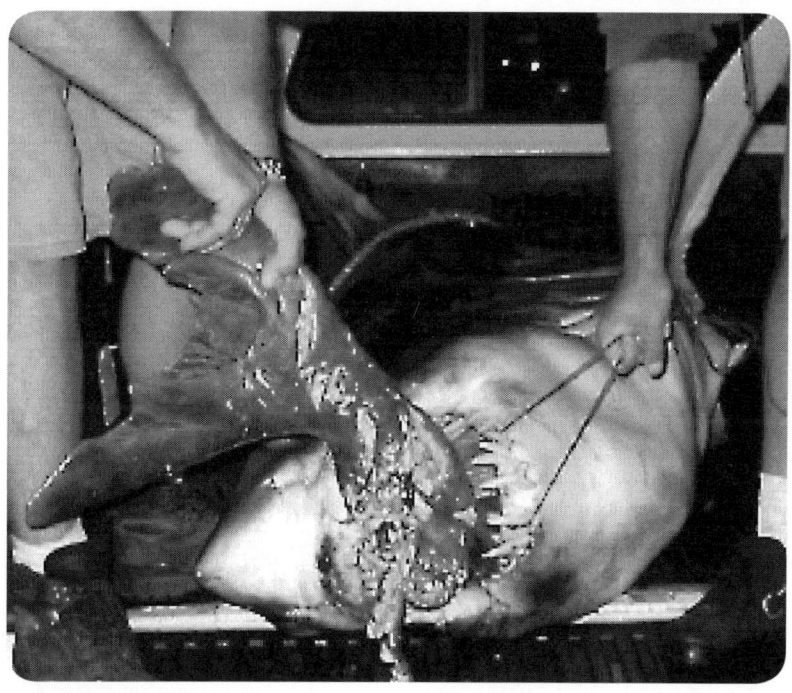

Makos eat a large variety of food. It's not uncommon to find assorted mammal parts or other creatures lodged within your catch. This 815 lb Mako had part of an elephant seal inside.

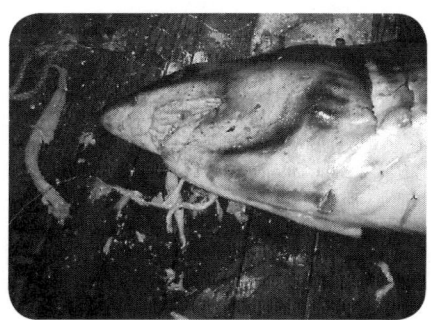 

An appetizer of eels was found inside this 387 lb Mako.

A piece of a seal was found inside this 601 lb Mako.

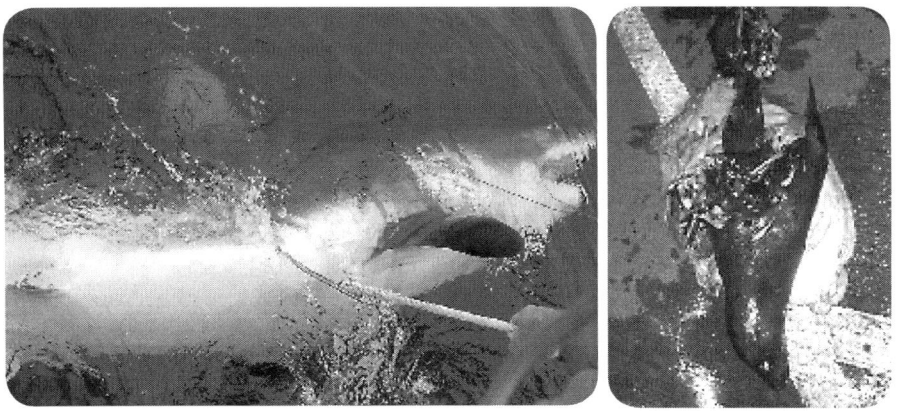

A seal was found in the stomach of the Mako pictured left

    Sharks are the only fish whose skeletal structure is comprised solely of cartilage; they have no bones. Since cartilage is lighter than bone, sharks have extreme flexibility. This flexibility gives Makos the ability to pursue prey, evade predators and to skillfully leap out of the water. Due to its beauty, aggressiveness, and jumping ability, the Mako shark is considered one of the great game fishes of the world.

Anatomy

Mako sharks have many characteristics that help distinguish them from other species of sharks. The Mako has a pointed snout, which no other shark possesses, and it's dorsal and pectoral fins lay completely perpendicular to its body (most species of sharks have downward-sloping fins). The Mako's tail appears almost bilateral and it possesses a keel. Makos have a lateral line that traverses their entire body; part of their sensory system, the lateral line allows the Mako to orient to movement and sound. The Mako has five gill slits, and large, dark black eyes. Makos are extremely hydrodynamic; their streamlined body makes them easy to identify.

Can you tell the difference between a White, Mako, Blue, Black Tip and a Bull shark?
With a bit of practice, the Mako's distinctive features make it easy to discern from other shark species.

1

2
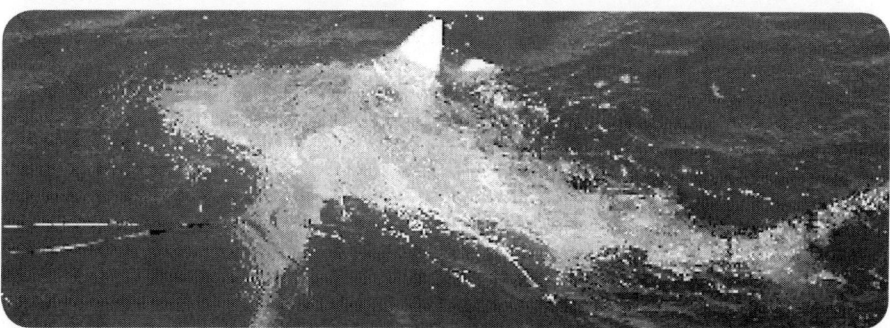

3

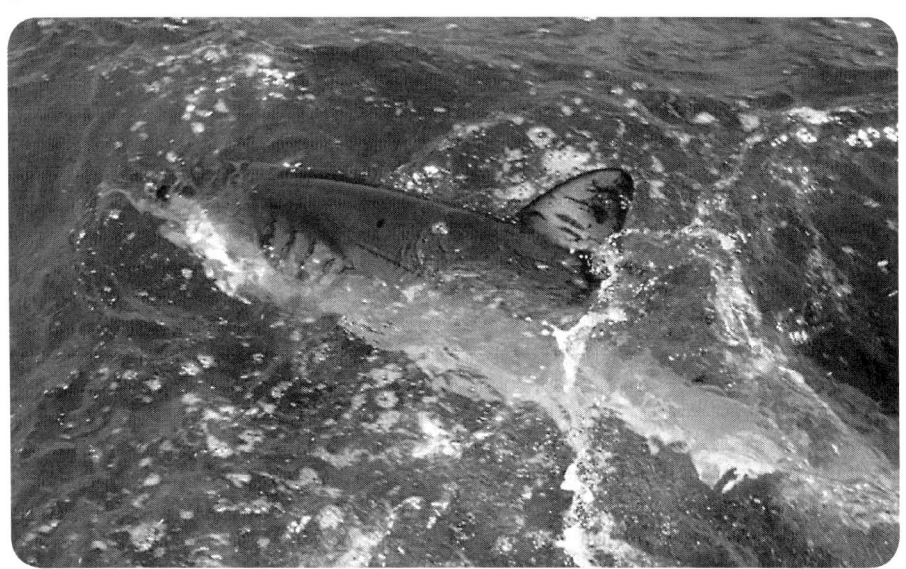

4

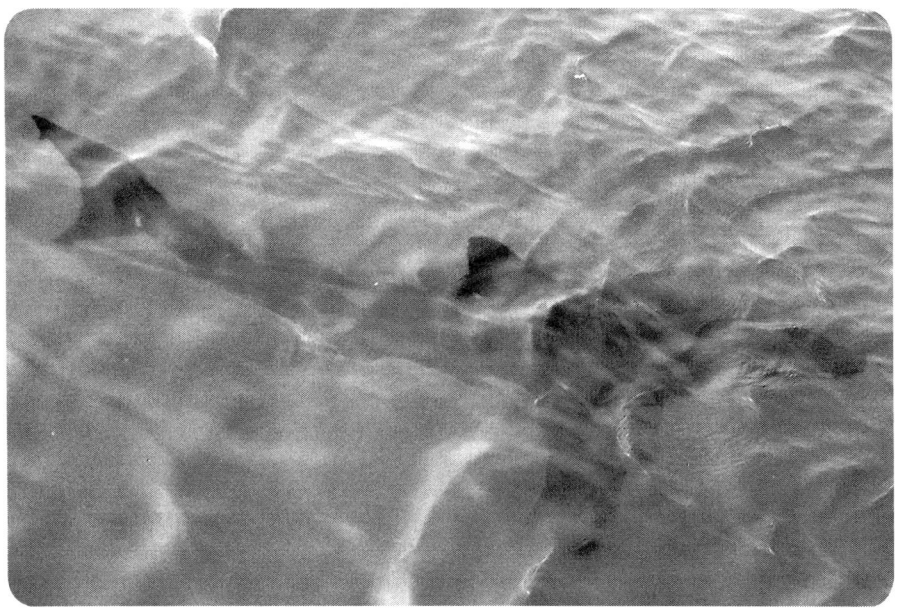

5

6

Number 1 is a Mako, 2 is a Bull, 3 is a Mako, 4 is a White, 5 is a Blue, & 6 is a Black Tip.

Male Makos have claspers (elongated pelvic fin edges), which are used for reproduction. Females have cloacae, openings that serve digestive and reproductive functions. Claspers are absent on the female Mako. Recognizing these differences can help you determine if your catch is male or female.

ANATOMY OF A SHARK

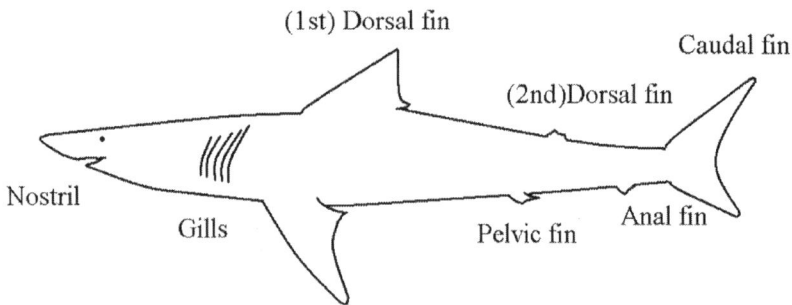

HOW TO DISTINGUISH MALE AND FEMALE SHARKS

JUVENILE CLASPERS   ADULT CLASPERS

MALE

FEMALE

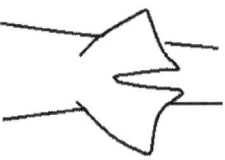

The skin on sharks consists of plate-like scales (dermal denticles) and a cartilaginous framework. When rubbed from the head to tail, shark's hide feels smooth. When rubbed the opposite direction (tail to head), it feels rough and jagged, like a saw blade.

Sharks have a never-ending supply of teeth, with five to fifteen rows inside their gums. Makos are unique; their teeth stick straight out.

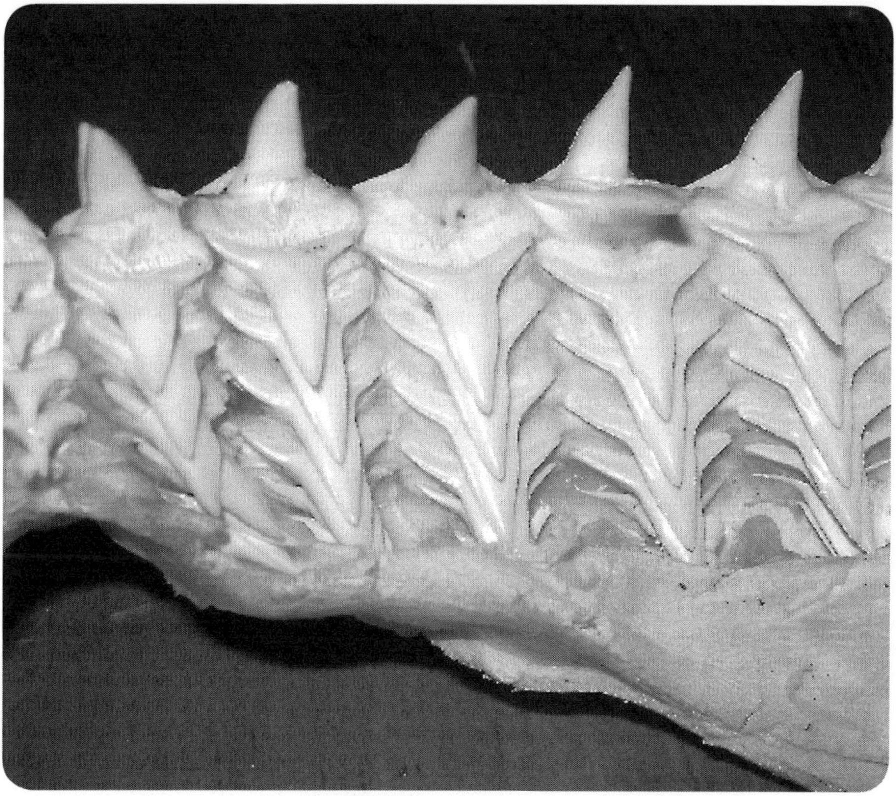

Rows of teeth

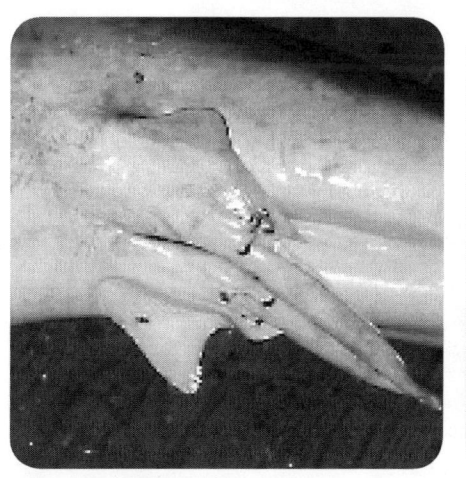

Male

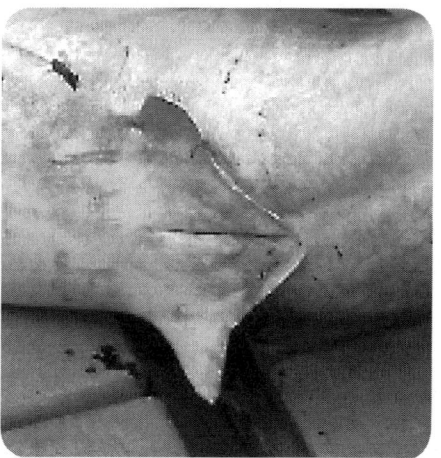

Female

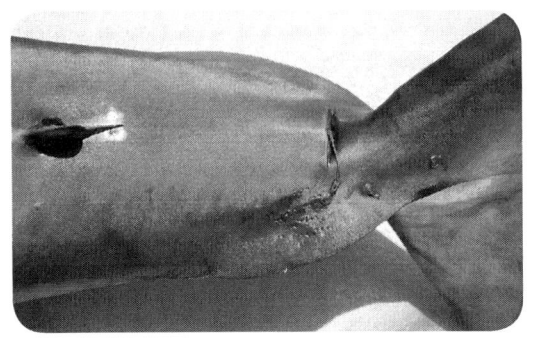

The tail on Mako sharks is also unique, because of its height to length ratio. The Mako's tail works like a propeller, producing maximum thrust with minimum drag. This unusual tail provides almost all of the Mako's propulsion. The Mako shark has a predominate keel at the bass of the tail. The keel is an easy way to identify a Mako from a Blue shark.

The Mako's highly-developed sense of smell occupies two-thirds of its brain. Makos can detect one part of blood per million parts of water using their ampullae of Lorenzini (small, sensory pores). This sensory network covers the shark's body, but is concentrated on the head and snout. The ampullae detect magnetic fields in close proximity to the shark, enabling the shark to locate prey and to deftly navigate through crowded waters.

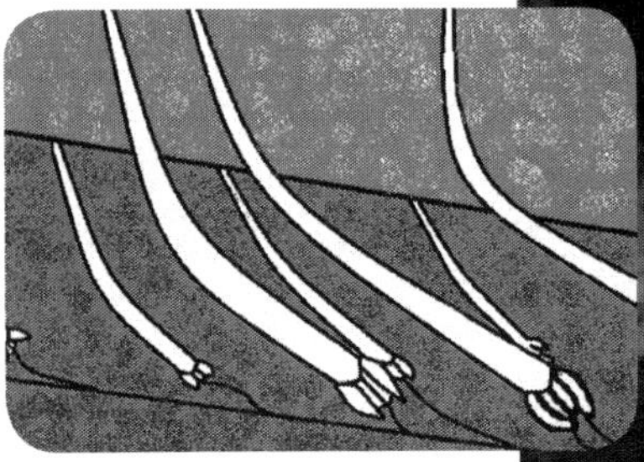

Ampullae of Lorenzini

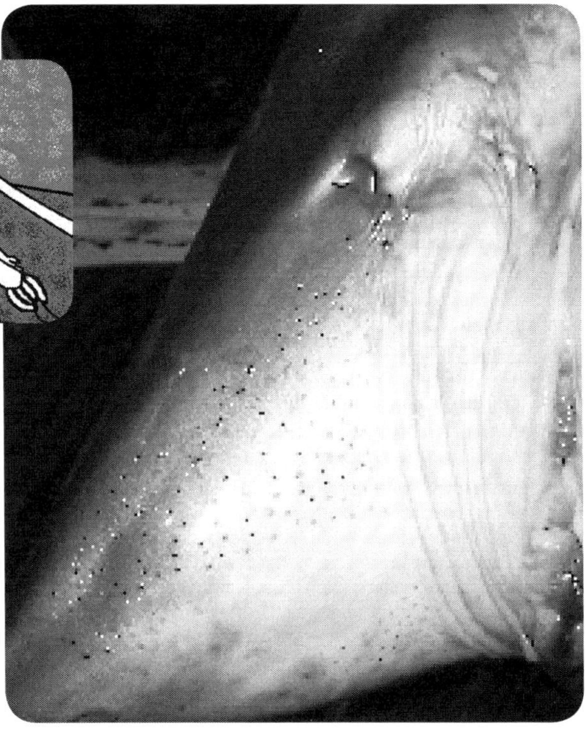

Ampullae locate even the weakest electrical impulses, like those of boat propellers, which attract Makos. The boat's battery connects to the engine, which grounds in the water, releasing electrical impulses that will attract the sharks to the boat.

Sharks also have keen hearing and detect minute sounds from great distances. Their sensitive hearing attracts them to low-frequency vibrations like a wounded fish or a ship's propeller.

Shark's sharp eyes amplify available light, allowing them to see at night or in low light levels. Their pupils expand and contract, controlling light intake. The eyes have a lens cover which slides over the eye for protection. This membrane slides over the eye just before sharks chomp on bait or other food. This is more noticeable in blue sharks than Makos, as Makos are more dauntless. Makos stare down their predators without fear.

Distribution

Makos live in warm waters worldwide and are most abundant off the coast of California. Many of the West Coast catches in the United States consist of juvenile fish; some adult-sized males are caught, but adult females are rarely taken. Large catches typically occur around the Channel Islands and outer banks of the Southern California Bight, at the beginning and end of summer. Nursery habitat utilization appears concentrated in the Southern California Bight area, primarily south of Los Angeles toward the Mexico-California border.

The Shortfin Mako has a very wide distribution, and can be found all over the world. It ranges from California to Chile in the Pacific, and from the Grand Banks to the hump of Brazil (including the Gulf of Mexico and the Caribbean Sea) in the Atlantic. Shortfin Makos are commonly sighted from Cape Cod to Cape Hatteras. In the eastern Atlantic, the Shortfin Mako ranges from Norway to South Africa (including the Mediterranean) and it is found throughout the Indian Ocean from South Africa to Australia. In the western Pacific, Makos range from Japan to New Zealand. In the central Pacific, it occurs from the Aleutian Islands to the Society Islands.

Habitat

The Shortfin Mako is a true pelagic species, primarily found in cool to warm waters. Makos are able to elevate and maintain higher body temperatures. While Makos live primarily in tepid waters along current breaks, they head into the cold, inshore waters to feed on hefty, energy-rich fish and mammals.

Makos are found in temperatures as low as 56 degrees Fahrenheit and at depths of 30-60 m. They have been recorded as deep as 740 m. However, Shortfin Makos prefer water temperatures between 56 and 68°F, where they are most often caught by sport fisherman. They migrate seasonally to warmer waters (proven by tag and release studies). Very little is known about the social habits of the Shortfin Mako, except that it is a solitary shark.

Behavior

Once you set a hook into a Mako, it's angry. Its survival instincts kick in, and all hell breaks loose. The Mako erupts wildly, rolling, shaking, diving, charging, and even leaping into the boat. Makos can leap as high as 30 feet out of the water. Once hooked, a Mako will often attack your boat. You'll feel like you've grabbed hold of the devil's tail when a Mako stares you down with its dark, pitiless eyes.

At the top of the food chain, these apex predators fall prey only to humans. Many falsely believe Makos are nocturnal feeders; long-lining day catches (vs. night catches) suggest the species feeds predominantly during daylight hours. While I've done my share of night fishing, most of my catches (especially larger ones) have occurred during the day. Makos feed on Mackerel, Bonitoes, Tuna, Marlin, Swordfish, Mola Mola, other sharks (including juvenile Makos), Squid, and the occasional marine mammal or Sea Turtle.

Not much is known about the mating habits of Makos, as they don't mate often, and it's yet to be witnessed. We do know though that when mating, male Makos grab their partner with their teeth, scarring them in the process. For this reason, female Makos have thicker skin than males.

515 pound female Mako with bite marks from mating.

Female Makos deliver via live birth, and can bear as many as 16 pups in a litter. The typical newborn pup measures 27 to 28 inches in length. Typical mature males measure about two meters (6.5 ft.) long; mature females measure about 2.75 meters (9 ft), somewhat larger than males.

Since pregnant females often abort embryos upon capture, few specifics about reproduction are known. There is evidence suggesting a three year reproductive cycle, although a two year cycle cannot be ruled out. Young are born after a 15 to 18 month gestation period. The age of Makos can be determined by counting the number of rings in their cartilage, similar to calculating the age of a tree. They reach maturity in four to six years, and have an average lifespan of 28 years.

Despite having two-thirds of their brain devoted to smell, Makos still have the ability to think and make judgments. These monster Makos don't become huge by being stupid. Spot a large Mako, and you will notice how it evaluates its situation and examines its locale. Makos are keenly intelligent creatures.

Dangers

The Mako's power, speed, aggressiveness and large raptorial teeth make it a very dangerous quarry that invites respect. Makos attack (and sometimes kill) those who hunt them, bumping, biting, and leaping into boats. Shortfin Makos approach with their mouths opens and swim in a figure eight pattern just before attacking.

This shark was hauled in alive during a tournament to keep it from being eaten by blue sharks and thereby disqualified. It bit the rail padding and tried to take a few chunks out of its captor, me.

Sharing the boat with a violent, thrashing Mako is an experience not soon forgotten. Makos are survivors and you have attacked them on their turf. Although the Mako is a fish, it is a potential killer.

THE MAKO SHARK

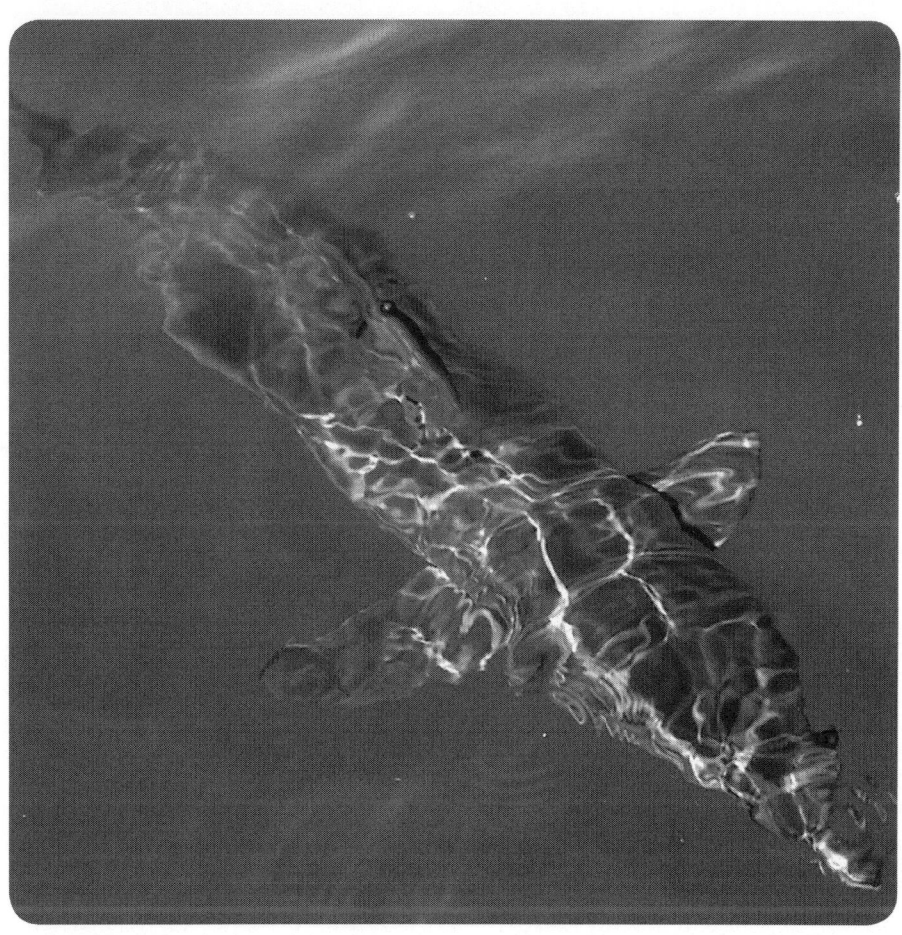

The Mako shark is a beautiful, fierce, fascinating animal. It provides a unique challenge for daring souls that seek extreme adventure. Knowledge of the Mako's habits and physiology, coupled with respect for its power and aggressiveness, will yield many successful expeditions.

SAFETY EQUIPMENT FOR BOAT AND PASSENGER SAFETY

Many foolhardy people grab the gear sections of a book like this and dash off to purchase fishing equipment, saving the safety equipment and electronics until last. Once they purchase expensive fishing equipment, they skimp on safety gear and or skip it altogether. Others think they are immune to hazards, or live in an idyllic world where nothing goes wrong. Seasoned boaters know that something goes wrong on every trip; it might be as insignificant as forgotten provisions, or as devastating as a serious injury. Equipment malfunctions, directions fail, people become ill, and boats break down. You can't afford to go all out on fishing equipment while ignoring safety.

Most shark fishing takes place far offshore, away from hospitals, and help. Offshore injuries and deaths happen every year. By following these important safety tips and procedures, you can minimize risks and injury.

IMPORTANT SAFETY EQUIPMENT

Coast Guard-Approved Safety Kit

When you purchase a boat, the dealer usually throws in some safety equipment: hand flares, a couple life vests, and a paddle. These are the bare basics required to be onboard by law. You don't want to stake your life on substandard safety equipment. Make sure all of your safety gear is approved by the U.S. Coast Guard (USCG).

Life Jackets

Purchase the very best life vest that you can afford, and again, assure that it is USCG-approved. You can't put a price on safety. Keep your life vests accessible at all times. Make sure your vests include a whistle and a light, as it may be impossible to scream over the wind, sea, and motors. A light can be visible two miles away, whereas without it you may not even be spotted 20 yards away.

The USCG has five types of approved Personal Flotation Devices (PFDs) ranked from Type I to Type V. The lower type numbers are best for offshore fishing. Type I vests are recommended when expedient help is unlikely, types II - IV are for when expedient help can be expected, and type V vests are specific use vests (work vests, sailboat harness PFDs, etc.). If you are taking seasick pills, are sick on a regular basis, have a low gunnel on your boat, or think you are extra vulnerable to fall over, I recommend you wear a Ultra IF Offshore Inflatable PFD. It is very compact, comfortable, and will inflate if you go in the water.

Emergency Signaling Light and Whistle for Life Jackets

It is critical to keep a high-quality emergency light and whistle attached to your life jackets at all times. Life preserver signaling emergency lights are intense, incandescent lights that are visible up to 2 miles away. I recommend purchasing one with a water-activation feature (automatically activates when submerged). A whistle will allow you to beckon aid in noisy ocean conditions.

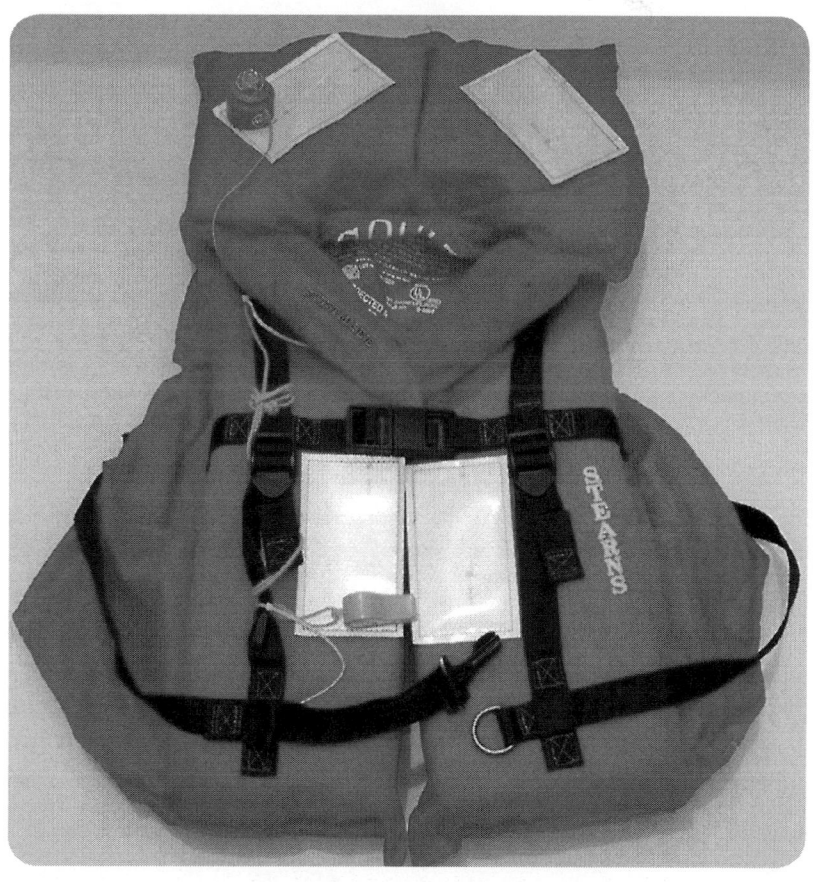

First-aid Kit

As you will likely use your first-aid kit numerous times, it is very important to get the best one you can afford. Since you can't run to the medicine closet or corner pharmacy, your kit must have more than Band-Aids. It must include emergency medicines, a variety of bandages and some tools. I also include a pack of sterile cloth diapers and duct tape in my kit.

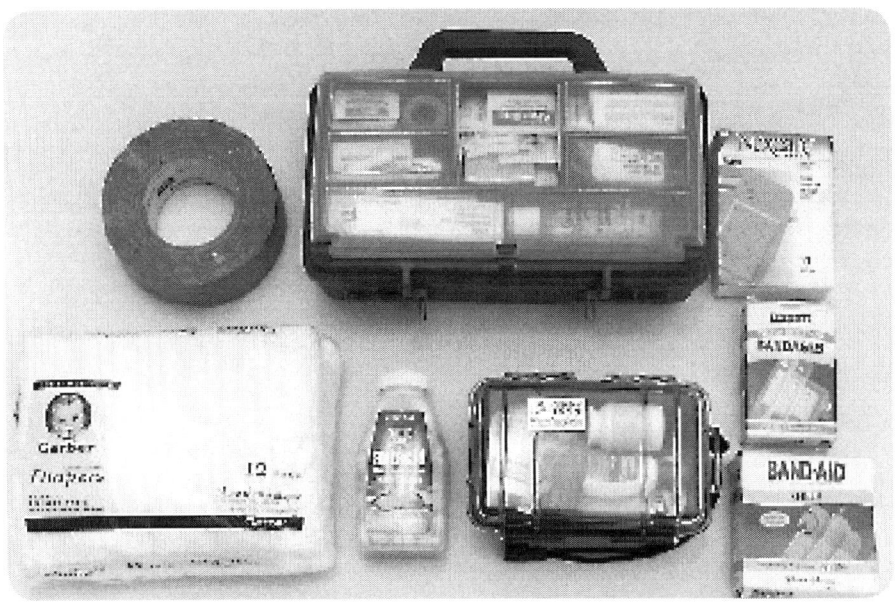

Your kit needs to be in a cool, dry place that is highly visible. Every crewmember must know its location. It is crucial that you familiarize yourself and your crew with the components of your first-aid kit before an emergency occurs. You can have all the supplies in the world, but when the time comes to use them, they'll do you no good if you are stumped about how they work.

Fire Extinguishers

Choose your fire extinguishers carefully and keep them handy. Keep one at the helm, one in the engine room, and another below deck. Choose a chemical agent extinguisher, as a clean agent may blow the fire around or make it worse.

Flare Kit

Choose a flare kit that can reach a very high altitude and is simple to aim and fire, so you can achieve the desired arc and placement of your flare. Without a high altitude (higher than that of a hand-held flare) the curvature of the earth could prevent your flare from being seen from a distance. Most kits come with three flares, but be sure to get some backups. Buy some practice flares and familiarize yourself with your flare launcher.

Several years ago on an excursion to "the Butterfly," a tuna fishing spot near San Diego, my crew and I assisted a stranded vessel due to thier deployment of a good flare. The ship had lost all power, was unable to electronically transmit a distress signal, and was in the rocks off the southern tip of the South Coronado Island. Because it was late and sea conditions were harsh, we had changed course from the tuna grounds, deciding to anchor up at North Coronado Island until daybreak. The marooned captain saw our running lights and shot up a flare. We would probably not have seen a hand flare, but because the ship was outfitted with good safety equipment, we were able to tow the shipwrecked crew to deeper water, and call the Coast Guard for rescue.

Hand-held Radio

A two- to five-mile transmission radio is an important piece of safety equipment that gives you direct access to emergency channels regardless of your position. Though it can be a good back-up, it is unwise to rely on your cell phone, as it may not get reception when you're far offshore. A hand-held radio will send out a much more reliable signal. Keep your radio charged and ready to be used in an emergency.

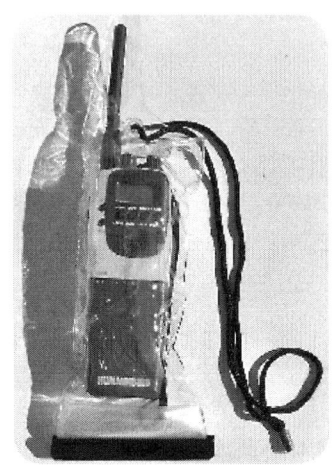

Emergency Position Indicating Radio Beacon (EPIRB)

Emergency position indicating radio beacons (EPIRBs) are the latest electronic safety advance. They can be used to call for help, and to indicate your location to rescue authorities. Costing from $700 to $4500, EPIRBs are invaluable for the safety and peace of mind they bring to your ventures.

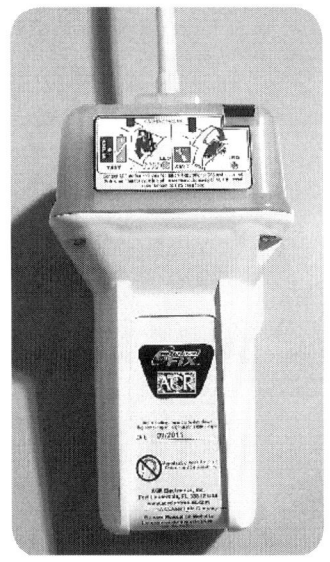

Choose an EPIRB with an internal GPS. These transmit your position along with your unique, digitally-coded distress signal, allowing rescue agencies to know both where, and *who*, you are.

Upon obtaining an EPIRB, note the batteries' shelf life (listed on the unit). If you purchased a boat with an EPIRB already aboard, be sure to re-register it in your name and your vessel's new name.

Life Raft

If you are going offshore, a life raft could become necessary. Be sure to provision your raft with food, water and emergency gear. A life raft is used "when all else fails." If you don't neglect your other safety equipment, hopefully you won't need one.

SEAWOLF
Why this is one of my choices?

I needed a boat that could withstand considerable punishment from the ocean and from me. Before purchasing the boat, I looked for small things that would be a big deal when at sea: a self-baling cockpit and the ability to upgrade with additional pumps, gear, electronics and safety equipment. Knowing my offshore adventures would be dangerous, a safe boat with high-quality construction topped my list.

The *SEAWOLF* Ultimate 30 (U30) is a Pro-Line 2950 Walk Around. Two 225-horsepower EFI Mercury motors push this boat to a top speed of 53 miles per hour. The boat holds 300 gallons of fuel for a range of 200 nautical miles, sleeps three with a full head, and holds 43 gallons of fresh water. The tuna tower -- a 360-degree padded platform (awesome for sight fishing) – was one of my first improvements.

I chose this Walk Around because it is wide enough to stand with your feet pointed straight out to port or starboard and has a 360-degree fishing capability; no obstructions hinder fighting a fish all the way around the boat. When you need to get to shark grounds quickly, like when you are in a tournament, the Walk Around has the dependability, speed and agility that will get you there first.

Other Equipment

This is not an all-inclusive safety equipment list. There are other important pieces you should consider, including: bells, foghorns, safety harnesses, throwable safety cushions for flotation, safety pouches for dry storage, radar reflectors, hand water pumps, a signal mirror, food or water storage, sea-sickness pills, chemical light sticks, cutting gloves, green dye markers, desalinators, and satellite phones.

SAFETY TIPS

Rule #99

On every excursion, as soon as people are on board, I immediately explain all the rules, regulations and saftey procedures that will protect them and the vessel. When someone does make a mistake, I jokingly say, "Don't you remember rule number 99?" Since most people can't remember all 99 rules, you should always keep an eye on them while they're onboard.

Crew Training

Whenever you are offshore, make sure your first mate knows how to run all the safety gear and operate the boat. If you are incapacitated, your first mate will be taking the helm, so you want to be sure he or she knows how to signal for help and how to utilize all of the boat's equipment. Both you and your first mate should take CPR and navigational classes prior to your first offshore adventure.

Autopilot

I love using autopilot on my boat, but if not used properly, it could be the deadliest thing on your boat. If you are going to use autopilot, use it responsibly. Always have someone on watch, and that person should not walk around the boat in any dangerous areas that might allow them to fall overboard.

On a trip coming back from Mexico to California, my mate and I were cruising at 28 knots with the autopilot on. My mate was sleeping down below while I was at the helm. I decided to relieve myself at the stern, rather than use the restroom down below. I stood at the stern watching the motors scream and the water rushing under the hull, it dawned on me that I could very easily fall overboard. If this were to happen, there would be no way to alert my mate, as he was asleep, and it could be absolutely disastrous.

Buddy Boating

When you make plans to go offshore fishing, see if you can make arrangements to buddy boat, or to communicate with someone else throughout your excursion. For your first few trips offshore, it is very important to pick a channel and stay in radio contact with somebody. To this day I buddy boat as often as possible. It's the safest way to go.

Float Plan

Prior to going offshore, implement a float plan. Plot out your adventure, and designate someone close to you to call the Coast Guard if you don't return at your appointed time. Make sure to provide your designee with all the information they will need to give the Coast Guard: where you were heading, when you should be back, how many people are with you, etc

Always have a float plan prior to your offshore adventures.

Safety Tale: Pair of Levis Saves Man's Life

On the water the unbelievable can happen, and knowing some simple safety information can save your life. The captain of a sport fisher told me an unforgettable story about an incident he had on a sharking trip about 20 miles offshore of Marina del Rey. After an exhausting day of heavy angling, they decided to head back to shore. The captain put the throttles down, heading for home. He assumed his mate went down below to sleep. An hour and fifteen minutes later, the captain arrived at the fuel docks and yelled for his mate to help tie up the boat. There was no answer. After searching the ship, and discovering his mate was not onboard, the frenzied captain alerted the Coast Guard, and sped back toward the shark grounds.

After reaching the grounds, two hours later, the captain found his mate floating in the water. Stranded in the open sea without a life vest, the mate took off his Levis and tied a knot in each pant leg. After cupping air repeatedly into each pant leg, he placed his chin over the crotch of the pants and stayed afloat until his captain returned to rescue him. Since he knew this simple method of converting a pair of blue jeans into a makeshift life vest, the mate was able to survive.

The captain was later able to piece together what had happened. When he throttled down to head for home, the sudden forward movement of the boat knocked the mate over the transom and into the water. This can happen quite easily; I've witnessed it myself numerous times. Wear your life vest or ultra inflatable PFD, always know where your crew is, and always have a backup plan!

The Best Safety Equipment

Before purchasing any gear that is foreign to you, check with your local dealer and your big game tackle store. Always speak to someone who knows what they are talking about, such as the store owner or whoever runs the shop. Don't be afraid to ask them to demonstrate how to use the equipment. Ask if there are any after-market products that might improve that particular product. If you have any doubts about a piece of equipment, don't get it. Being comfortable with your gear is very important.

Which of the equipment pictured here would be best to have if your ship was going down?

1. Type I foam life jacket

2. Type III vest

3. Type III vest

4. Type II foam life jacket

5. Waterproof ditch bag with radio, whistle, and flairs

I wouldn't hesitate to pick items 1 & 5 if I were going down.

Preparing the Boat and Crew for the Adventure

If you're a captain of a boat, then you already know that preparing your boat is a job in itself, no matter how small the trip. Turning switches, valves, and doors, opening hatches, unloading the truck…you know the routine. Now you're stepping into the big leagues; preparing for a big game fishing trip is infinitely more work. You have additional equipment to load and much more planning to do.

Each crew member must be assigned specific tasks on your expedition.

You must find the right person for each shipboard duty and you must assure that all tasks, no matter how minor they might seem, are completed. It gets crazy on the open seas; this is no place to drop the ball. Each crew member will carry out numerous duties which aren't set in stone. Situations arise where you have to switch tasks and adapt plans at the last second. Your crew needs to know how to react when the time comes. Foreseeing your crew's abilities and adaptability can make the difference between having a pleasant day catching a monster, and having all hell break loose. With the right organization and teamwork, you'll have a safe and enjoyable day out in the water.

BOAT AND PASSENGER SAFETY

Nothing can have such far-reaching consequences or ruin a trip more quickly than neglect of boat and passenger safety. From the moment you decide to fish, safety must take a prominent position in your mind. Realize that you are embarking on a dangerous venture, and that things can (and often will) go wrong. Prepare yourself, your ship and your crew to minimize risks, and equip them to handle any emergency that may arise.

Emergency channel is 16.

Finding Shark Grounds

Big game fishermen are overachievers who live to walk the edge of extreme. Shark fishing, an extreme sport that gets inside a person's soul, takes a special combination of guts and planning to pull off successfully. Battling these huge sea monsters will make your adrenaline pump, your heart race, and will feed your spirit like nothing you've ever experienced.

Finding good sharking grounds is an art unto itself, not something you can just decide the morning of your trip. Landing monster sharks requires research, planning and of course, a little luck. You can blindly set sail and pray you land a monster, but if you put in the effort to find good grounds, your work will be rewarded with the impressive catch you seek. Before setting out, you'll need to put careful thought into a number of important geographical, weather and water conditions, all essential to finding your quarry.

Water Temperatures and Current Breaks

Checking temperature maps (satellite images, available on the internet) will positively help you find good shark grounds. Good information is available at *www.terrafin.com*. Be sure to print your map once you've located the right one. It will be important to have this information with you. With the map, you need to look for water temperatures, current breaks (in conjunction with the locations of the continental shelf), and high spots. This is one of the most important bits of information to consider when looking for sharking grounds. Sharks don't just swim around aimlessly hoping to come across food. They are on top of the food chain, constantly on the hunt. Sharks maximize their fuel efficiency by looking for food in the most optimum spots. Understanding the significance of water temperatures, temperature breaks, and current breaks, will make finding that optimum spot that much easier.

Water temperatures are a key factor in shark fishing. Larger Mako sharks are normally caught in 58-68°F (surface temperature) waters. Warmer water tends to net smaller Makos, but don't rule out the possibility of larger Makos inhabiting it. Cooler water tends to bring in blue sharks. In cooler waters, you'll have to do more sight fishing to avoid hooking blues.

Satellite images are your best friend. They show the water temperatures of large areas. If you use satellite images prior to getting on the water, you can plot an area that is likely teeming with fish. My catches increased significantly when I started using temperature maps.

Temperature breaks occur when two bodies of water with varying temperatures meet (going from cool water to warm water, warm water to cool water, warm water to warmer water, etc.), or where an eddy is present. An eddy is a body of water that has broken off from a strong front. A temperature break can vary within a couple tenths of a degree and a couple of degrees.

A current break is a body of water similar to a freeway, almost like a river in the middle of the ocean. Current breaks range from several yards to hundreds of yards wide. Though you can't see a current break on a temperature map, you can estimate where they will appear. Current breaks appear around temperature breaks.

Foamy current break

Greasy or calm water current break

Weed line current break

The more drastic the temperature break, the more likely it is that a current break is near. Current breaks can run for miles in length. Sometimes fish are found in the current break, and sometimes just outside, on one side or the other of the current break. In places where a cold body of water meets a warm body of water, you should check for life. Check the cold side and the warm side. I typically start my drift just on the edge of the cold side, then go into the warm side, mainly fishing the warm side of the current break. I start on the cold side because Makos swim to the edge to see if there is anything to eat before going back into the warm side.

At the beginning and the of the season find the current breaks, fish the warm side and you will hit pay dirt! The season starts in April and ends in November.

Where current breaks are formed or come together, they can create a weed line that goes on for miles. Kelp paddies get caught between the two masses of water, and bait fish tend to hide under the kelp. Bait fish attract larger fish which, in turn, attract sharks. Always look under kelp paddies for large game fish or sharks. If the current break looks good, set up on one side or the other of the weed line or break. Sharks swim along these breaks searching for an easy meal.

Bait fish hiding beneath a kelp paddy

Safety

For safety's sake, be sure to look into weather warnings and predictions such as: swell, tide, wind, atmospheric pressure. You can find reliable weather warnings on VHF radio, TV, the news, the Internet (*www.noaa.gov/*), and by looking at trends. Read the sky. This is an instinct, but can also be a learned art. Reading the sky is important because it helps you determine the next day's weather, and make safe, responsible choices. For example, if you forecast poor weather conditions for the next day, you probably won't want to go too far offshore; you might find it safer to stay in the short banks. If you predict a pleasant day ahead, going far offshore may be an option. Reading the sky helps you plan an enjoyable and safe trip.

There is much truth in the old adage, "A red sky at night is a sailor's delight. Red sky in the morning, sailors take warning." A red sky at night indicates that the following day will probably be fair and pleasant. You can tell a night sky is red when the clouds are red, the sky has a red tone to it, or red haze is evident. A red sky in the morning indicates that winds may increase and conditions can become stormy and unpleasant, even if it was calm in the morning. Ideally you want to go out after a nice, red night sky, though nothing is ever guaranteed.

Atmospheric Pressure, Winds and Currents, and Swells

Atmospheric pressure is based upon low and high fronts that move over your region. Atmospheric pressure affects the physical properties of the water, which affects the behavior of everything within it. A barometer is a handy tool. When the barometer shows a drop in atmospheric pressure, you may experience bad weather and poor fishing conditions. An increase in atmospheric pressure generally indicates pleasant weather and good fishing conditions.

It's a good idea to view a wind analysis map for the day before your trip. These are available at no cost on the internet. Look at a 12 hour loop of the previous day's wind direction and strength. The pattern from the day before your trip will usually be consistent with that of the day of the trip. Use your wind analysis in conjunction with a temperature map to plan a great fishing site.

Keep the morning wind and current direction in mind, because it will come into play on your shark drifts. For example, the winds could be offshore for a few hours, and then change to onshore for the remainder of the day. You don't want to drift one direction and later drift in the opposite direction, back through your slick into the same area you've already covered. I live and die by the wind direction for my fishing tactics and patterns. I plan my days and drift locations in accordance with wind direction before I even stop the boat.

Once on a drift, if you find yourself drifting slightly off course, use the wind and the sail power of your boat to your advantage. Allow the wind to push you along in the direction you want to drift. Do this by making minor adjustments to the helm wheel and forcing the boat onto the desired course.

Sunny Days vs. Cloudy Days, Water Colors, Attributes, Sunlight, and Light Conditions

Understanding water color and its significance presents a considerable advantage for salt water fishermen. The sun, clouds, and water depth (in shallow areas) affect the color of the water. On sunny days, expect to be able to see deeper into the water, and to have good sight fishing. On cloudy days, you are more likely to spot finning sharks, but water visibility is poorer. Sight fishing from the tuna tower will give you a bird's eye view into the water. Always wear polarized sunglasses for sighting; these increase vision over the naked eye.

It's best to look for cobalt water. Cobalt water provides the best visibility, and has paid off for me on numerous occasions. However, you can't rule out good fishing in other colored waters. In the summer of 2003, pea green water dominated the California coast. It continued as far as a one-day range could get you, and there was no relief for months. During all the tournaments that summer, we were forced to fish in this pea green water, though we never would have fished it if we had a choice. Contrary to the water conditions, it turned out to be a great fishing year for everyone.

Tides

Good tidal movement enhances any fishing day. Conversely, a lack of tidal movement and current can pretty much guarantee a lousy trip. Also, fish tend to bite on the high tides on the west cost and the low tides on the east coast.

Tidal movement is caused by the gravitational interaction between the earth and the moon. Gravity causes the oceans to bulge out in two directions – in the direction of the moon, and on the opposite side. While this is happening, the earth is rotating, so high and low tides occur twice a day. The gravitational forces of the moon and the sun both contribute to the tides. Moon phases determine the strength and height of a tide's pull.

Spring tides (not related to the season spring) occur during the new moon and the full moon. These especially strong tides occur when the sun, the moon and the earth are in a line. Neap tides (especially weak tides) occur during quarter moons. They occur because the moon and the sun are perpendicular to one another in their relation to the earth.

Tides can vary in height from 1 foot to 50 feet, depending on your location. On the east coast, tidal movements going out from shallow bays and lagoons push bait fish into deeper waters; sharks will wait to feed in the deeper waters. You should set up on the incoming or outgoing tide, ready to catch the sharks as they come to feed. You want to be in position just before the high tide; you might miss a good fish bite (when the fish are biting heavily) if you wait until the tides begin moving to set up.

The general consensus on the west coast is that the high tide is a great feeding time for sharks. During high tide, sharks tend to feed closer to the shore. Almost all of my big catches are done during high tide.

Sharks go to shallow water at night and to deeper water during the day. When there is a full moon, expect a lot more night feeding than usual. On the other hand, no moon at night can produce better fishing the following day.

I advise purchasing a tide book and keeping it on your boat. Some of the new GPS systems have built-in, real time tide charts.

Check Reliable Sources

As a final preparation before your trip, you should talk to other people who have been on the water within the last week. When you talk to others who have recently been on the water, make note of where they caught fish. Look at the water temps from the day they were out and perhaps you will notice a temperature trend.

Checking local shark fishing internet message boards is also a great way to find the action. While you're on the boards, it is a good idea to post your plans. Message boards are a great way to get advice and meet fellow shark fisherman.

When you get to the fuel or bait dock, check with reliable sources for grounds. Be prepared to make a change right until the minute you leave the harbor. Ask the bait salesman or gas station attendant, or any other knowledgeable sources, "Where's the bite?" They might tell you a particular location, such as where they commercially caught or hooked half a dozen fish. You might find this spot is not far out of the way that you intended to go. You definitely should take a look at any spots your sources recommend.

Choosing your spot(s) should be based upon a combination of all the above information. Always have multiple fishing spots in mind, never set your plans in stone, and always have a "Plan B" and a "Plan C."

Let the Hunt Begin!

The actual adventure of getting out there and performing the hunt across the open oceans is the most exhilarating part of the trip. The ocean is alive, a being with a temperament, with good days and bad days. The ways in which she moves and operates are just awe-inspiring. Unbelievably crazy things happen when you're out there on the water. Just being on the ocean makes for exciting, unpredictable days.

With your destination established, set your GPS coordinates for a route. Be aware of current breaks, water temperatures, the continental shelf and high spot locations. Use your GPS with chart plotter to find water current location and cartography, including C-map technology on your fishing grounds.

GPS with chart plotter (I highly recommend Garmin brand GPS systems). Use for water current location and cartography, including C-map technology on your fishing grounds. Color fish finder/sonar: Look for temperature breaks, signs of life below the surface, temperature, and the thermocline.

Thermocline

Understanding the dynamic balance between the ocean's layers can improve your catches. Thermocline is a water layer with a sharp temperature change which separates the cool, abyssal water from the warmer, surface water. During summer, the sun heats the surface water of the ocean, often to 80 degrees or more. This floats over a layer of more dense, colder water. Thermocline is the thin layer between these two layers where the water temperature drops substantially. The warm water thermocline is usually above 400 feet. Most bait balls will be found above the thermocline, and where there is bait, there are sharks.

When deep sea fishing (500 fathoms or more) for Makos, the thermocline is of little importance, considering it can be over a hundred feet below the surface of the water. Watch the thermocline on your fish finder while drifting, occasionally it will be near the surface. If it starts showing bait balls, add a weight to drop your bait just above the thermocline.

In order for your fish finder to pick up thermocline, you will need to set the gain high so it can pick up the minutest changes in the water.

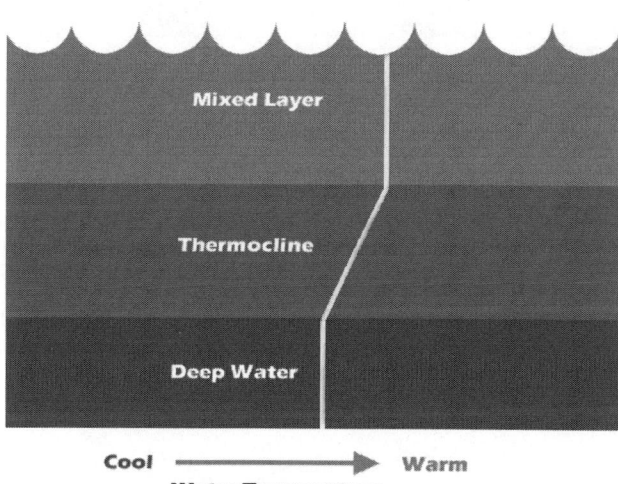

I prefer *not* to use downriggers and weighted bait, as I like to fish as sporty as possible and without extra gear. Chunking fish to the boat is a preferable method rather than a trial, lucky hit on the thermocline. By chunking pieces of mackerel, they will go deep in the waters and below all thermocline. The only time I use downriggers is when trolling for threshers.

Signs of Life

Look for signs of life both above and below the water. Above the water, look for birds, sea lions, dolphins, whales, bait fish, and other fish. Below the surface, use your sonar to look for meter marks (bait, bait balls or other large fish).

As stated above, signs of life include birds, sea lions, dolphins, whales, bait fish and other fish. A flock of seagulls is a sure sign that baitfish may be in the area.

If you see a free-jumping or finning shark on the way to your route, you might want to bait that fish or hang out and try the area.

The Continental Shelf, High Spots and Fathom Curves

The continental shelf is a submerged body of land that lies along the shore lines, 10 to 100 fathoms below sea level. On average, it extends up to 40 miles out. Once you surpass 100 fathoms, there is usually a steep, vertical drop between 100 and 600 fathoms, which I call the 500 fathom curve. Beyond the 500 fathom curve, the shelf begins to gradually slope down to the ocean floor. In some areas, the continental shelf creates deep water canyons that run directly into the shoreline. Continental shelves typically signify a drastic change in current and water temperature.

A high spot is a prominence of land arising from the ocean floor. High spots normally extend to just below the surface. A typical high spot is within a few hundred feet below the surface.

The bottom of the ocean is rich in nutrients. Near continental shelves and high spots, the water currents from the deep (the bottom of the ocean) flow along the bottom and then hit the continental shelf and rise upward, bringing nutrients toward the surface. Bait fish are attracted to these nutrients. The bait fish attract larger fish, ultimately luring in the top predators, sharks. Because of this, high spots and continental shelves are popular fishing spots. I regularly scout the 100 and 500 fathom curves.

On the west coast, the continental shelf is commonly passed up because many fishermen think they have to go to the outer high spots to find good grounds. On many occasions I've come across abundant sea life on the shelf, along with some of the biggest free-jumping and swimming sharks I've ever seen.

If a high spot produces big catches, after you drift off to the point it stops producing, go back to the high spot where they are biting.

Night Fishing

Night fishing is particularly popular on the East coast, where reaching the continental shelf and good sharking grounds is a lengthy venture. On the West coast, the continental shelf lays only a couple of miles out, so day trips are more tenable.

In my early sharking days, night fishing was introduced to me by Fred Archer, a notable fisherman from the East coast who has written a book on shark fishing. I'd heard from many sources that fishing at night was popular and fun. Since I could leave Friday afternoons after work and go out sharking all night, I decided to experiment with the concept. When I first starting shark fishing, I was so excited to get out on the water that I couldn't wait until Saturday morning to get started. My experiences with night fishing were unpleasant: falling asleep in cold, rough waters by the shipping lanes, having the watchman fall asleep at night, being out in the colder part of the day, disappointing catches. While we did catch sharks at night, my catches were rather small. There were blue sharks (not my quarry) in abundance, but only small Makos. I'm not saying that larger Makos don't come to feed at night, but I only caught small Makos and found the whole experience unfulfilling.

I continued night fishing for a few years until I began to question myself. Shark fishing is dangerous enough, and why would I want to increase that danger? There are almost no other boats out at night, and this is not wise in case of emergency. The boat's deck was more slippery because fish blood that had dried during the day was now wet again. There was no visibility. It wasn't until after I quit night fishing that I learned the advantages of sight fishing. When I started sight fishing I stopped hooking blues, and started landing the big Makos I was after.

Another problem I have with night fishing is that no matter how much lighting you muster, you can't see adequately. Powerful deck lights and underwater lights don't get the job done. I added four floods under my swim step (in addition to the two floods in back on the hardtop), one on each side, and one on the front all the way around the boat. I had powerful squid lights to attach to my rod holders or submerge in the water. I was king of the world with

this setup, able to light up everything, but it wasn't practical. Excessive lighting expends battery power; if you have a generator you've got an advantage in this respect. Lights reflect off the surface of the water, so they don't help you see deep into the water, much like turning on bright headlights in fog.

It took me a long time to stop night fishing; I really enjoyed the added excitement of being out there on a small, lonely craft, hunting wild sea monsters in the dark of night. However, after some hair-raising experiences, the dangers became apparent to me and I knew I should stop. I can't think of many sound reasons for night fishing. Lighting isn't an issue during the day; visibility is good and sight fishing reigns supreme.

> TIP: Don't make plans to night fish on your private, small craft — especially if you are just learning how to shark fish!

Adapting Your Plan, Enjoying Your Trip

Preparing for a trip is a lot of work and costs time and energy. You must do your best to ensure an enjoyable day. Sometimes you'll find that even with the best research, preparation and planning, nothing's coming to the boat. Don't be discouraged, it happens to all of us. If a spot isn't producing after a couple hours, or if you get to your grounds and find someone is already there, move on to "Plan B," or "Plan C."

Once you've chosen your route, pick your best spotter (best at spotting fins and free jumpers) to ride shotgun. This step is important and often overlooked. When you pick someone, make sure he is able to read the water well and is knowledgeable of the ocean. Also consider their ability to differentiate fins of different animals. You don't want to stop the boat every time you see a seal, Mola Mola, or porpoise fin.

Use common sense when near other boats, and always keep appropriate distance. If an area is crowded, or things don't look "fishy," move on to the next spot on your list. If you decide to stay, always fish upwind of the other boats. This will prevent the other boat from fishing your slick.

With good planning and execution, you will probably find favorable grounds. They may be somewhere other than your initial destination. If you find worthy grounds while en route, it's fine to investigate it or give it a try before moving on. While proceeding, you should constantly compare your boat's GPS location to your temp map location.

After the Trip
After every trip, record a detailed, extensive trip log including records of any fish you caught. Store your notes, along with a wind and temp map printout, in a log book for future reference. Many computer programs are available to help record data about your trips. Compiling trip information may help you locate good fishing spots, based on previous reports. I have referred back to logs of my big catches on several occasions. I find new hunting grounds based on information from previous successful hunts: tide, temperature, catch locations compared to the month the catch was made.

I've found the following information helpful for logbook inclusion: trip date, people on the excursion, starting location, starting time, trip time (across the water), fuel consumption going to your destination, miles to and name of fishing locations, any events that occurred en route, what was caught/released, miles drifted, other events, mileage, and fuel consumption of the trip back. Also record the remaining amount of fuel, and a list of things that broke or malfunctioned on the boat during the trip.

Landing Monster Sharks
Fishermen have to fish; the hunt keeps our blood flowing. I enjoy and get excited over every catch from the littlest fish in a stream or pond to the big fish that inhabit the ocean's depths. I've caught just about every type of fish that swims in the ocean.

I've had many exciting and memorable seafaring days. My expeditions have gotten better and better through the years, largely due to hooking up with good people, learning to read the seas, finding good grounds, and using the right equipment. Experience has been my greatest instructor. I am passing my many years of experience on to you.

I hope this information will give you a leg up on your voyages. You can start right away using information that took me years of fishing to learn. When you are able to find good grounds on your own, it is definitely more rewarding. With these tips and some experience, you should be able to find better spots and have more options once you get out there. The road signs on the ocean's endless swells are less concrete than highway markers, but once you know what to look for, you'll find them.

Equipment

Choosing the right gear for shark fishing is a daunting task. From the onset, it is critical that you select high-quality equipment. With so many products and choices, you need a solid guide for making reliable purchases. Years of experience with equipment has helped me create this list of necessary, dependable shark fishing gear.

Guns
I prefer to avoid using guns for a number of reasons. This is big game fishing, not buffalo sniping in the Wild West. In my early days, I used to go out there with bang sticks and all manner of artillery. Since then, I've learned that it's not necessary to kill an animal with a gun. To me, using a gun is a dishonorable way to dispatch any fish. It flat-out doesn't give the fish a chance.

The use of guns is also prohibited by the International Game Fish Association (IGFA) because it is not considered sporting. Imagine the distress of landing a world record fish, and being automatically disqualified. Since these rules govern almost all shark fishing tournaments, it is best to avoid their use in your regular excursions. Treat your regular fishing days as if they were tournaments; practice IGFA rules and you will be properly prepared to set records and take home big prizes. You certainly don't want to make tournament day the day you try to learn how to boat a prize-winning Mako without a gun. (For the IFGA rules go to www.igfa.org)

Shooting a Mako gives a false sense of security. Fifty percent of the sharks I've shot at point-blank range (and presumed to be dead) did not die from the initial bullet wound. The brain and heart of a Mako are so small that it's almost impossible to accurately strike these vital organs with a bullet. There's nothing more terrifying than dragging a "dead" shark onto your deck and having it explode in a miraculous resurrection.

Guns are very dangerous to carry onboard, and should only be used if you have the proper training and knowledge to use them safely. Keeping the safety on provides extra security, but the only true "safety" is to unload the gun, the safest method of all. With some guns, knowing if the safety is actually on can be a problem. Usually, the owner of a gun is the only one familiar with it, and able to accurately access the status of the safety feature.

Never pass a loaded weapon around. You can lose track of whether or not the safety is on. The likelihood of a gun accident increases with each transaction.

Guns on a boat present all manner of senseless danger. It's not prudent to be wielding firearms on a slippery deck or in hectic situations. If your gun is dropped or falls off the seat, it could discharge and cap someone in the rear.

A bad shot, or a shot that ricochets off a shark, can put a bullet through the boat's hull and into one of the fuel cells, igniting the fuel. The fuel is stored in the rear of the boat, usually where you are boating the shark. Most boats carry 150 to 1,000 gallons of fuel which could potentially ignite in a huge fireball.

If you're determined to use a gun, I recommend using a Glock. Since it is made of plastic, it holds up well in the water. Be aware, however, that there is no safety feature on the Glock.

For safety, be sure each person handling your gun has taken firearms training (and passed a firearms test). When handling your gun, always assume it is loaded and ready to fire. Always lock the trigger or weapon carrying case when you stow your gun.

> TIP: A revolver is always loaded and chambered with live rounds. A semi-automatic is chambered only after you pull the slide back. After shooting a live round, it automatically feeds another live round into the chamber. After taking the clip out of the gun, the chamber still has a live round in it which needs to be manually removed.

The captain is responsible for everybody's life on the boat, including his own. As a boat captain, I always have peace of mind when I am the only one on board handling a firearm. This puts all the responsibility on me, and keeps me from having to rely on the judgment of anyone else.

Gaffs

Gaffs come in many shapes and sizes. There are numerous types of gaffs out there, and everyone claims that they have the best one. Only a select few are able to handle a 150-1000 pound shark. Fixed gaffs and fly gaffs work in conjunction with one another. You should have *at least* one of each with you at all times. However, no matter how good a gaff you have, if you don't know how to properly place it into a fish, it could be disastrous.

I like the Accurate Shark Hunter Fixed Gaff because the hook and handle are able to withstand tremendous force. Mine took eight years of abuse before I had a problem with it. When it finally broke — the hook broke off the handle while gaffing a 300 pound Mako — Accurate replaced it for me at no cost. I highly recommend this Gaff.

Fixed Gaffs
1. Accurate Shark Hunter Fixed Gaff
    This gaff features a six-foot handle with a six-inch hook and is great for reaching out far! The handle and hook strength are heavy duty.
2. Aftco Fixed Gaff
    This gaff features a six-foot handle with a six-inch or eight-inch taper-tip gold anodized hook. Its slim, tapered shaft provides for easier gaffing. It is easier to maneuver in the water, and can react faster to actions of the fish; but thin walled aluminum is easy to bend.

Fly Gaffs
1. Accurate Fly Gaff
    This tournament fly gaff features a six-inch hook. It is very strong but it's also very hard to get it to penetrate the thick skin of a Mako. This gaff will most likely not bend on you.
2. Aftco Fly Gaff
    I modified this big game fly gaff to accommodate for big sharks. The fly gaff features a 12-inch hook Pro Point and is made with marine grade stainless steel. This sturdy gaff

hook will not bend in use, but I have broken two of their handles and had to mod those too. I recommend getting one of these gaffs only if you can mod it.

Right: Top Shot Fly Gaff
Below: Accurate Fly Gaff

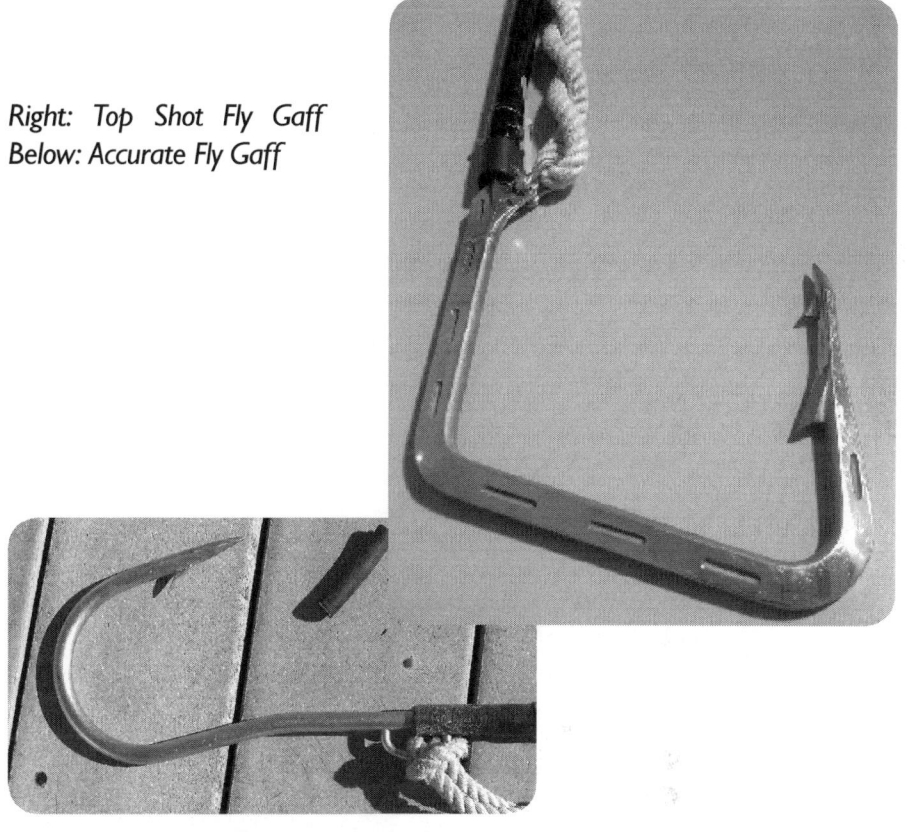

3. Top Shot Fly Gaff

This fly gaff features a 12-inch hook Pro Point and is made with marine grade stainless steel. It comes in five different sizes. This sturdy gaff will not bend in use. I recommend getting one of these gaffs.

The stainless steel point on the Aftco Fly Gaff is very sharp and can be easy to bury into a large Mako. I have used this gaff on all of my big Mako catches. While this gaff can be easy to sink into a fish, it is just as easy to bend (if it's placed wrong, or the fish is too big for this non-reinforced gaff) and come out of the fish, as the picture on the next page illustrates.

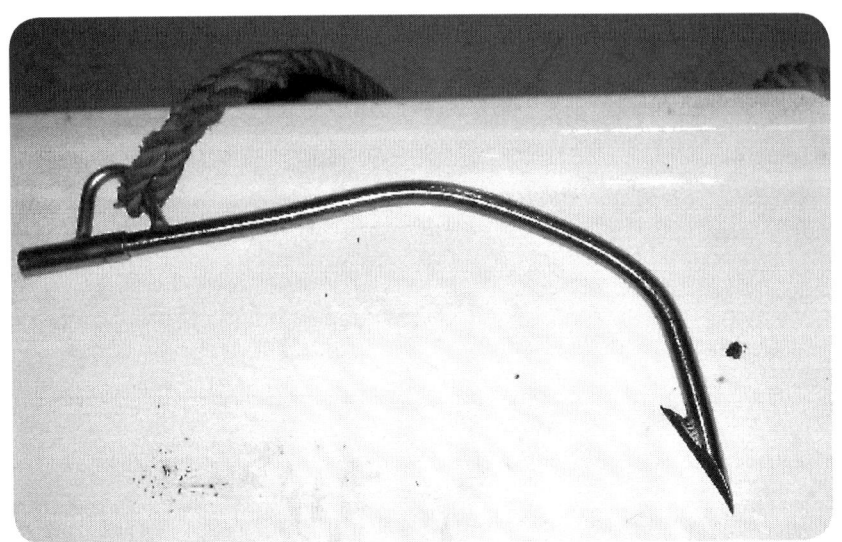

This Aftco Fly Gaff is not reinforced and it did not have the strength to hold the fish.

SAFETY

- Gaffs are one of the most dangerous pieces of equipment on your boat.
- If you purchase a fly gaff and are not familiar with how to operate it, ask the shop owner to demonstrate it for you.
- If the crew does not already know, teach them the procedures and precautions for usage
  before letting them use or rig this equipment themselves.
- Keep the protected covers on the hooks until you are ready to use them.
- Always have gaffs tied off and ready to use. You do not want to find yourself rushing at the
  last minute, running with a gaff in your hand, and possibly striking one of your mates.
- Do not tie your fly gaff on the fighting chair or hand rails; use the outside cleat instead.
- Be careful when holding the fly gaff rope after sticking a shark, as you can get severe rope burn, dislocate your shoulder, or even get pulled overboard. To prevent rope burn, always wear gloves when operating a fly gaff or handling the rope.

- If you miss the fish with the fly gaff on the first try, be patient, re-rig the gaff and bring the fish to the side of the boat again.
- If you stick a fish with a straight gaff before you hit it with a fly gaff and the fish is getting away (and taking you with him), let go of the gaff.
- When you stick a large shark using a fly gaff, make sure you are not standing on the rope or the wrong side of the rope.

Puncture wound from a gaff without a saftey cover on the tip

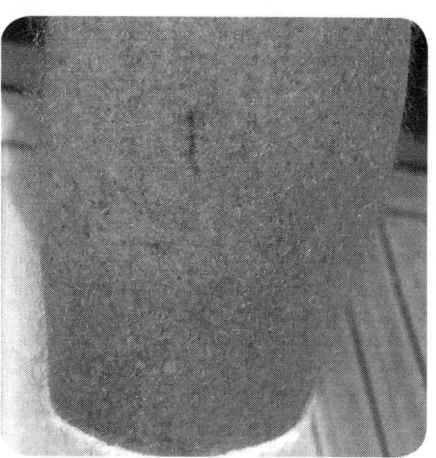

This scar was the result of a Fly Gaff through the leg

GAFF STORIES

Dead Man

I was at a local boat supply shop and observed a man at the counter asking for the manager. In his hands lay a broken, twenty-dollar gaff he claimed to have purchased a few weeks before. When I saw the gaff, I knew it had been under an enormous amount of stress, no less than a 100- to 150-pound beast. When the manager arrived, the man (who I immediately nicknamed "Dead Man") asked for a replacement gaff, stating that he'd broken the gaff hook trying to catch a 45-pound halibut. When I heard this, I knew he was lying through his teeth.

"Wow! That must have been some halibut," the manager replied in disbelief. Dead Man simply stood their laughing. The manager agreed to replace the gaff.

Brace yourselves, sure enough at this point, Dead Man asked if he had wire leaders (for shark fishing) in stock. He had not gaffed a 45-pound halibut as he'd claimed; he was wrangling toothy critters that will eat you, given half a chance. He was doing this with some of the cheapest equipment you can buy, equipment that is inadequate for the job. Dead Man is the guy who won't ask for professional advice, and will only learn through trial and error. He's in for some hard lessons.

One Gaff, Two Gaffs, Three Gaffs, Four

During a high stakes tournament where I thought I had everything under control, the unexpected happened — one gaff after another malfunctioned, turning a controlled situation into a mad minute. With each gaff I swung into the beast, I feared more and more that we would lose this tournament-winning Mako. Had it not been for preparation and backup gear, the shark would have surely roamed free. After a one and a half hour fight, we managed to catch the Mako, winning second place in the 2001 Mako for Dollars tournament.

The first gaff we used was the Accurate Fly Gaff tied on the port side. When I went to stick the fish, the gaff malfunctioned, since it was not properly rigged by a crew member. The hook had disengaged from the handle prematurely, and did not penetrate the fish.

The second fly we used was an Aftco Fly Gaff, which was tied to starboard. It went into the shark like butter, presenting no problems. Immediately I decided to swing another gaff into the shark, because one fly gaff isn't secure enough for such a large fish. While sinking the Accurate Shark Hunter Fixed Gaff, I was shocked when the hook broke off of the handle.

Down to my last gaff, I grabbed an Aftco fixed gaff and buried it into the shark. Normally, I would not use this particular gaff on such a large Mako. Since it was the only one quickly accessible to me, I had no choice but to try using it. Had this not been a tournament, and had I not been so worried about the fish getting loose, I would have simply re-rigged my Accurate Fly Gaff and used it. I guess we struck a nerve, because the shark went crazy at the port side, thrashing and rolling alongside the boat. As the shark is rolling, it wraps the Aftco fixed gaff around itself, crushing my fingers against the boat as I held the gaff. As the pain became unbearable, I had to let go of the gaff.

My mate grabbed the Aftco fixed gaff. I told him to let go of it, because the shark was going down. He let it go, and sure enough the shark went under the boat. Because the Aftco gaff was tied to the starboard side, and the fish had gone under the boat, I told my mate to get to the other side of the fly gaff rope (so he would not get caught in it). As he jumped to the other side of the rope, the fish unexpectedly came up to surface from the port side, miraculously with the bent Aftco gaff still intact. My mate grabbed the gaff and told me he had a good grip on it. I yelled for him to hold it in place, while I put a tail rope on the shark. After getting the tail rope on, I applied a head-rope, tying the fish to the port side, forward cleat

As you can see, our gaffs went through a lot of stress, and we were very fortunate to finally catch the Mako. Luckily, I was prepared with two fly gaffs and two straight gaffs on board.

Aftco Fixed Gaff bent into a U-shape. While this gaff is not meant for handling such large Makos, we could not have done without it.

Knives

Knives are an important part of shark fishing. Below is a comprehensive list of some of the best knives and their purposes in shark fishing.

Shark Killing and Bleeding Knives

The Ka-bar 1272 stainless steel hunter's knife is sturdy, strong, and heavy enough to drive into the head of a Mako with ease, splitting the cartilage and paralyzing the fish. It features an 8-inch long blade that is 1.5 inches wide. I also use this knife to cut the gills and bleed out the fish. This knife is the preferred knife of the U.S. Military.

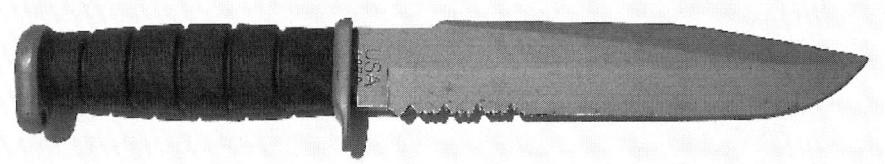

The Ka-bar 1272

The 9-inch Dexter Russell double-serrated edged shark knife is a cheaper alternative to the Ka-bar. A few drives to the head will knock a Mako out. It's ideal for slipping in between gill slits and cutting the plates, to bleed out the Mako.

The Dexter Russell Shark Knife

Cartilage Sawing Knives

The Stanley FatMax drywall knife has a non-slip, rubber handle. Like the Dexter Russell, its jagged blade and sharpened tip make it ideal for cutting cartilage.

The Stanley FatMax

Bait Knives

Rapala Soft Grip 4-inch and 9-inch blade stainless steel knives are light, sturdy, and maintain a sharp edge making them solid enough to drive into the top of your chum bucket (to start cutting a hole) without breaking. They also do a great job of cutting bait.

Mundial 8-inch butcher's stainless steel knife is great for cutting larger sized bait. Due to the unique shape of this knife's tip, driving it into any large bait is easy. Rather than sawing through the bait, this cuts with a thrusting motion.

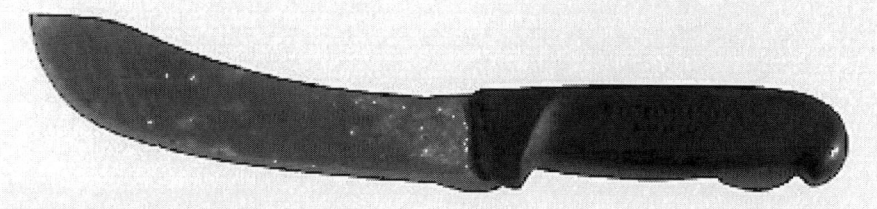

Mundial butcher's knife. Note the unique shape of the tip

Mako Carving Knives

These knives are intended strictly for carving the Mako. Do not use them for *anything* else, because you need your knives in tip-top condition for something as intensive as cutting through a shark. I use the Forschner Victorinox 8-inch breaking knife and the high-carbon, no-stain, 12-inch Mundial knife. As long as you have one eight-inch knife and one twelve-inch knife, the brand doesn't really matter. I like these knives because they are very sharp and sturdy. The 12-inch knives are very long and wide, and able to cut through the toughest shark meat and even cartilage. The 8-inch knives are like a scaled down version of the 12-inch, but used for cutting smaller parts of the shark. For more information on what these are used for, see "Butchering the Mako, page 171"

From top to bottom, diamond steel knife sharpener, Rapala bait knife 6", Rapala bait knife 9", Mundial butcher's knife 7", Forschner butcher knife 8", Forschner butcher knife 12"

Knife Sharpener

The knife sharpener is an important piece of equipment that is often overlooked. I recommend Industrial Diamond's Eze-lap knife sharpener.

Knife Care and Safety Tips

- For extra security, equip a stainless steel fillet glove.
- Whenever you have knives onboard, keep them in the sheath or in a mounted knife holder.
- When you are finished using a knife, put it away in a secure place. Do not leave it on a seat or anywhere else where someone may be reaching for something else and accidentally jam the knife into their hand. Also, be sure not to place it on the gunnel, or anywhere else that it can move around freely. Boats are usually rocking; leaving a knife loose is turning it into a potential projectile.
- Always know your knives' location.
- Before putting your knives away, be sure to clean and dry them off properly. Wash and dry them with a rag, then wipe them down with WD-40 to prevent rusting. A properly cared for knife can last a lifetime; lack of adequate treatment will greatly reduce the lifespan of your knives.
- Keep them covered!

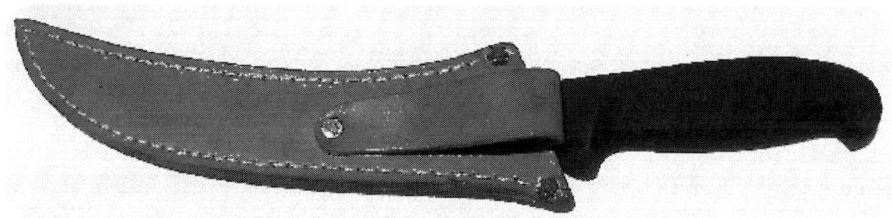

Tailers

Tailers are designed to subdue a shark. Typically, a tailer is used for one of four reasons: subduing a shark, holding a shark to measure it, removing a hook from a shark, or tagging and releasing a shark.

When I first started shark fishing with my uncle, he kept a tailer on his boat. After using it numerous times and seeing the danger it posed, I opted not to purchase one for my boat. I went many years without using one, but once I got back into shark tournament fishing (where a minimum length fish may win a tournament), I realized that I would need a faster and better method to measure fish without hurting it.

I chose the Aftco Tailer because it is ideal for holding small fish. This tailer is not recommended for fish larger than 100 pounds. According to Aftco, "When used on a fish that is to be released, the tailer is more effective than a lip gaff, and it minimizes injury to the fish." While this statement may be true, it neglects to mention that this increases the risk of injury to the operator of the tailer. Upon disengaging the tailer be careful, sharks are flexible enough to contort their entire body and bite their own tail. If your hand is on the tail of the shark, you may find yourself in a compromised position.

The Aftco Tailer

Safety
- When releasing the cinch cable off the tail of a shark, you will have to grab the shark's tail with one hand and release the pressure of the cable with the other. Remember that sharks are flexible enough to bite their own tail. I've seen sharks do this on numerous occasions.
- A tailer alone is not enough to keep a shark under control. You need to subdue it from both ends, stretching it out as much as you can, making it as immobile as possible.
- Just because you have a shark on a tailer, never throw it on the deck alive. You will not be able to manage it; a tailer alone does not give enough control over the shark.
- If you are a novice shark fisherman trying to catch and release a shark, you might want to have your mate use a tailer to hold the shark steady, while you maneuver safely to remove the hook from a shark's mouth.

Tag Sticks

The primary purpose of tagging is to track the migration and growth patterns of fish. You tag each fish with a uniquely-numbered card on which you record the shark's data. Later, if the fish is recaptured, the tag can be removed and sent in for scientific study. For every tag card, there is a tag with the same number.

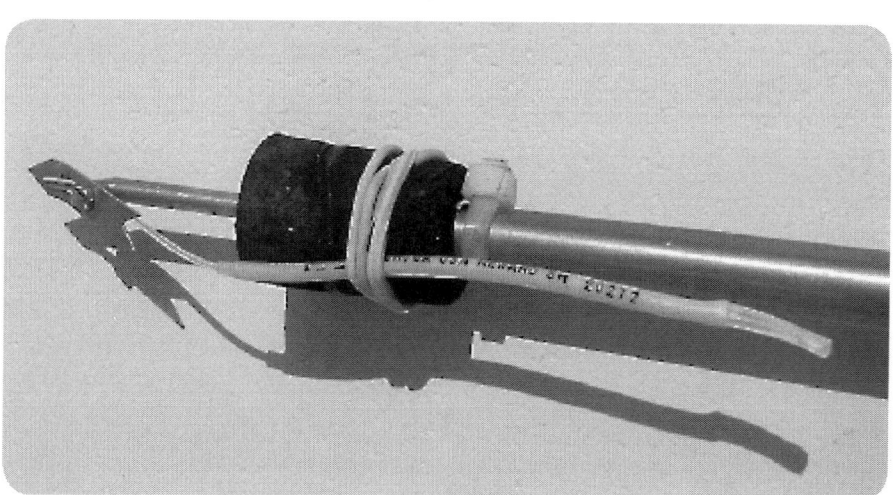

The tag card asks questions such as sex and size of the fish, and where it was tagged. This helps marine biologists learn more about these creatures, which ultimately helps us as shark fisherman as well, but only if the fish is recaptured and the tag sent in.

A tag stick has a sharp metal tip on it, in which a tag is inserted. The stick is thrust into the fish, the tag which has a unique number is inserted into the fish. The card containing the same number as the tag is sent to marine biologists to file; when the tag is returned these specialists can study the fish's migration and growth between captures. If you ever see a tagged fish, please make your best effort to remove the yellow spaghetti tag, report the information, re-tag and release the fish. Send the old tag to researchers, along with the new card.

I keep tags and a tag stick on my boat at all times. As a shark fisherman, I feel it is my responsibility to participate in the study of these sharks. Sport fishermen are the forefront of this project. After you send in those tags there are literally hundreds of people working behind you. Your participation is an integral part of these programs' success.

Obtaining a Tag Stick

You can either purchase a tag stick or make your own. If you choose to make one yourself, contact any tagging organization for tags and a tag tip which you can place into an old broomstick handle to make your own tag stick. I have been using an Aftco Tag Stick for many years and it has never given me any problems. The Aftco Tag Stick costs around $50.

Release Sticks

This is one of the most important pieces of equipment you can have before you start shark fishing. A release stick is used to remove hooks from live sharks. If for no other reason, the amount of money it will save you on hooks you retrieve with it should convince you to not skimp on one. It's also better for the shark that you are able to remove a hook from its jaw instead of simply cutting the wire. Without a release stick, the only way to remove a hook from a shark is with a set of pliers. Of course this requires your hands be extremely close to the shark, which is very risky. A release stick gives you a six foot distance from the shark, and is considerably easier to operate with than a set of pliers.

Since I release almost all of my catches, it is comforting for me to know that I can remove the hook from the shark's mouth before I release it.

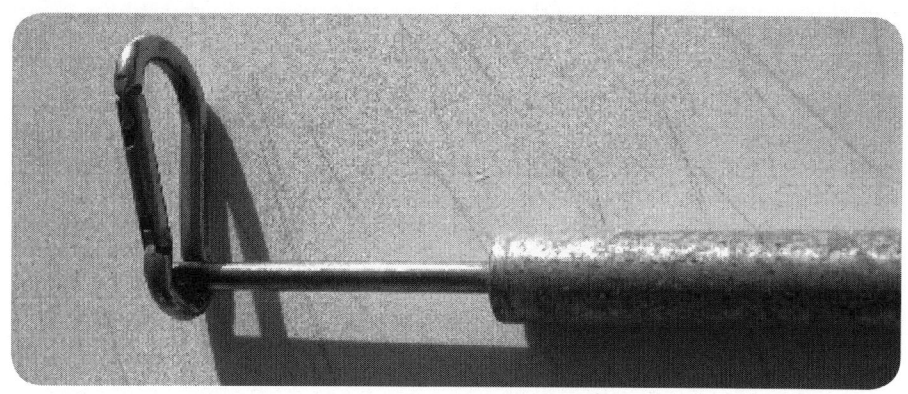

Six-foot Accurate Predator Release Stick
All of the paint is worn off due to heavy use of this release stick.
I can't imagine what it would be like to not have one of these onboard, considering how much I use it.

Safety
- When attempting to remove a hook (once you clip the leader in), if the shark makes a run, let the wire leader and line slip through the release stick clip. Once the shark stops running, unclip the release stick from the line, and then let the angler re-fight the shark. If you try to hold onto the leader while the shark is running away, you will *not* win. The shark will run more often than not.
- Take extra precaution not to let the wire leader wrap around any part of your body, or lie anywhere on the deck where someone may step in the loop.

Fish Bats

Bats are a must to carry onboard. The pupose of a bat is to knock the fish senseless, and then bleed it to death with a knife. This is usually done while the fish is tied alongside the boat or off the swim step. I use an Aftco aluminum fish bat. It has a short handle, allowing you to swing it with only one hand.

Sometimes you may think a fish is dead, and bring it in only to find out it is still alive. Other times you will want to bring a half-conscious fish into the fish holed (obviously the fish has to be small enough for the fish hole). In tournaments, you want to bring a fish in as soon as possible to prevent it from being mutilated by other sharks thereby disqualifying your catch. In tournaments, guns are not allowed, so it may take a while to kill the fish. In either case, you will need to bring the fish onboard as soon as possible.

Let's assume you've just caught a fifty pound halibut, and it's now on your deck flopping around. This fish surely packs a wallop, and you definitely want an effective means of fighting it. Some people would try knocking the fish out by stomping it with their foot. This is not very effective, and it only angers the fish more. The bat is much more effective for dispatching the fish.

Swinging a bat at a shark can be very exhilarating, but it can also be dangerous if you don't take necessary precautions. If the people you are entertaining on your boat ask you if they can start beating on a shark with your bat, make wise decisions about who you will and will not allow to use the bat. Once someone has a bat in their hand and starts vigorously beating on a shark, rage and adrenaline *will* kick in. Because of this adrenaline, the operator of the bat may start swinging wildly, hitting the side of the boat, or, even worse, you or another member onboard.

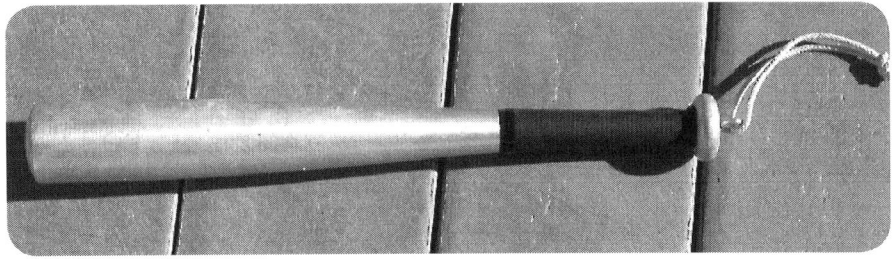

Aftco Aluminum Fish Bat

> **TIP:** If you are entertaining a guest, such as a client or out-of-town relative, you do not want to leave them with an image of you acting like a psycho. Be a bit more calm and reserved when using a bat. Save the madman routine for your buddies.

Ropes

Ropes are among your most important pieces of equipment. The four dock lines that you use in your boat are sufficient for tying a Mako alongside the boat. You need one rope for the head and another for the tail. Often times you will need to retie the head. Instead of removing the old rope and redoing it, it is more convenient to slip another over the original head rope. A fourth rope can be used for numerous reasons, such as securing the shark, making a slip handle, or tying the middle of the body. I'd recommend your dock lines be at least 15-25 feet long.

Harpoons

The way I catch Makos, there's no need for a harpoon. But who doesn't have the desire to run up to the bow of the boat and spear a harpoon through a free-swimming shark? I was raised with tales of Moby Dick, which implanted a fantasy image of adventure on the high seas. On my wild, imaginary adventure, I am at my boat's pulpit with a harpoon tightly gripped in one hand as the boat crashes through the swell and the spray comes up in my face. My eyes are focused on the beast as I see a fin approaching faster and faster. My heart pounds so loudly -- I think my mates can hear it! My arm tenses up on the harpoon, and every muscle in my body goes tight as I prepare to slay the treacherous beast. As the boat climbs over the top of the fish, I expend every ounce of energy from my body into my arm as my harpoon dives deep into the beast. As the beast makes a ferocious run with the cable flying violently, I hear the screeching of brakes as the cable goes taut.

That sound is actually reality hitting hard. This isn't what would happen; I would be bringing the fish alongside the boat before driving a harpoon into it. Not much sportsmanship in that. Back to reality...do I own a harpoon? Nope. Do I want a harpoon? You bet, but I don't plan to ever get one. Harpoons are not permitted by IGFA regulations, and they're just not sporty. Don't get me wrong, I don't think owning one makes you a bad person. Swordfish and sharks meet their fate by the razor sharp tip of a harpoon on a daily basis. I personally don't want to live with the fact that I slaughtered a magnificent creature in such an unsporting manner. I find gaffing a fish is more rewarding, as it gives the fish a chance to get away, making your kill a true accomplishment.

Rods & Reels

When you're going to battle, your weapon of choice is crucial. If you don't bring a high quality rod and reel for monster Mako fishing, you might as well stay on the beach. There is a reason I buy the best reels on the market, and it's not for bragging rights — there are record fish weighing 1,000 pounds and more out in the ocean just waiting to be caught. When I started fishing, I was skeptical about purchasing such expensive equipment, and figured I'd skimp my way through. After many bent rod guides, burned out reel drag washers, and broken leaders, I knew I needed to step up to the plate if I wanted to catch these beasts of the sea. Even the smaller sharks were a challenge without quality gear. After purchasing high quality rods and reels, I caught more and bigger fish. Now I'm armed to the teeth and ready to catch whatever the ocean throws at me, runt or beast.

Rods

While I have rods for all species of fishing, only about 50 percent of them are custom built. The other 50 percent are the highest quality factory made rods, the best that money can buy. Since my custom rods are all non-rollers, I added Fuji SIC/USG (silicon carbide) guides, because the heat/friction dissipation created by the line on these guides, is the best on the market. If you thread three feet of 30-pound test line through one of the stainless steel eyes of your rod (non-roller guide), then hold it on each end and jerk the line back and forth (with the eye as the pivot point) as fast as you can for 15 seconds, the line will most likely either fray or break. Now, if you were to run the same test using a Fuji guide, the guide will get hot, but the line will stay cool and will not fray or break. This is especially important since Makos can have speed bursts of up to 60 miles per hour.

Reels

When I first started shark fishing, I used a Penn Senator and Daiwa Sealine conventional star drag reels. Star drag reels are great for getting into the sport. They are cheap and it's very likely that you already have some of these accessible to you, but along with their low cost is a huge sacrifice in quality. The drag washers on these reels are about the size of a quarter. Because of their small size, they heat up very quickly and cause the reel to jerk and bind up. They also tend to get very sticky and rough along the surface.

Lever drags are a better choice. One of the most notable features of lever drag reels is the lever itself. The lever gives you the ability to adjust the drag setting with ease. Some reels even have the drag settings labeled on a plate directly beneath the lever itself. Unlike star drags, lever drags have numerous, metal and composite washers (more than five times the size of a star drag washer), each with a very high heat dissipation rate. In addition, they are concealed inside the reels, so they are virtually waterproof. Some of the Shimano Tiagra series reels are so advanced that they have hydrothermal drag systems built in. I purchased one of these as soon as they came out, and to this day it is one of my favorite reels.

Before you get too excited, be warned that lever drag reels can cost up to five times as much as star drag reels. However, if you can shell out the cash, you will have a lasting investment. You will probably be able to keep these reels throughout your life and hand them down to your kids one day.

One day while out shark fishing with my 12 year-old son, Dillon, I decided to teach him the difference between two different types of drag systems. I let him catch, tag and release a moderate sized Mako with a lever drag reel. He had fun toying with the Mako.

Later that same day, a large blue shark swam up to the chum slick, and Dillon begged me to let him catch it. I agreed on the condition that he brings it to the leader, to tag and release it. After watching him catch the Mako with such ease using a lever drag reel, I thought

maybe I was spoiling him. I threw him a curve ball and tossed him a 25 pound star drag outfit that we use for bait fishing, and told Dillon to catch the shark with this rod. He baited the shark and the fight began. Dillon fought the blue for about 30 minutes, trying to bring the fish to the boat. He was successful twice, but the shark made a run for it each time. Frustrated, Dillon said he wanted to give up. I reminded him of the promise he made to me that he would bring it to the leader, so he reluctantly went back to work.

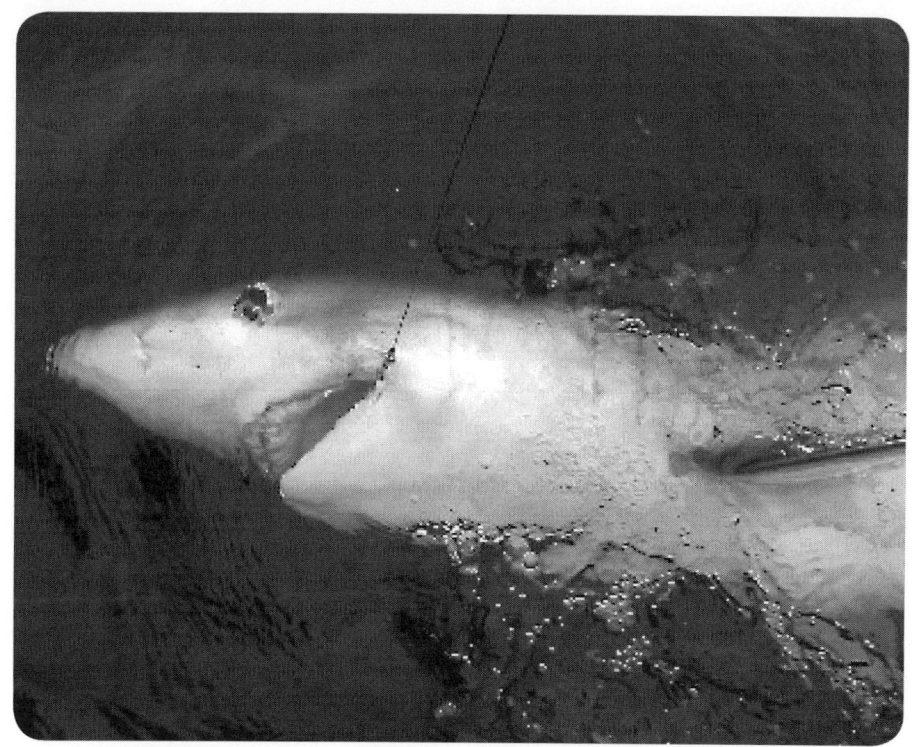

After fifteen minutes, he successfully brought the fish close enough to grab the leader and set a tag. Once the tag was set, the fish took another run, pinning the rod to the rail. Dillon didn't give up, and brought the shark back so we could properly release the fish.

After the exhausting ordeal, he could clearly see the difference between a star drag and lever drag. I felt bad because I gave him the cheaper gear, and it seemed to me like he didn't enjoy the battle. On the contrary, he was so excited about his 200+ pound catch, that he called up several friends to tell them the story. He had a great time and learned some valuable lessons about choosing proper gear.

Comparing Drag Washers Visually

The drag washers pictured below are from various reels. Note the size and width variations, remembering that larger drag washers have higher heat dissipation rates, giving these drags the ability to stand up to bigger fish. Comparing the width of the star drags to the lever drags is like comparing the width of a piece of cardboard to the clutch of a car.

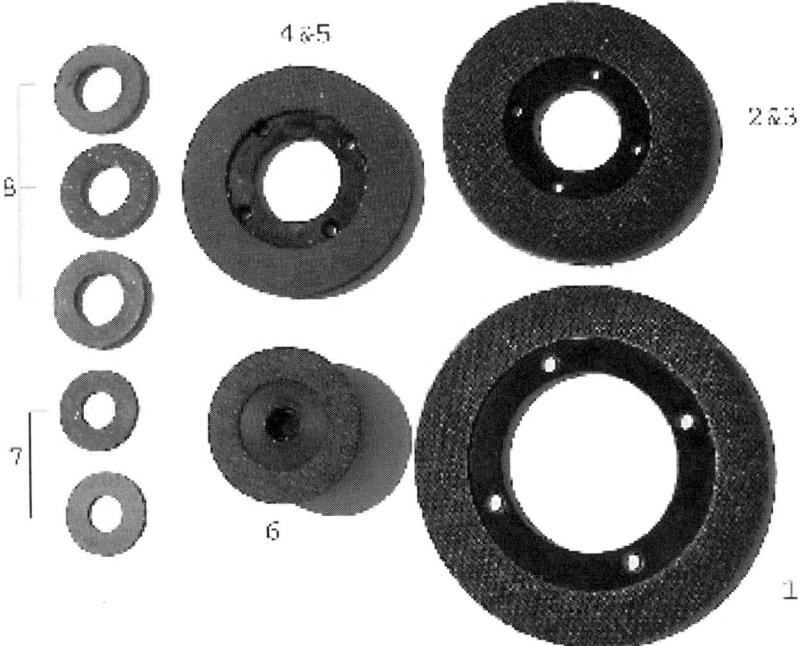

Drag washers (above), and their appropriate reels (below)

Reels and the Washers They Use
(Numbers refer to pictures above)
1. Penn 130ST- 4" diameter drag washers (x2)
2. Penn 80STW- 3 1/4" diameter drag washers (x2)
3. Penn 50SW- 3 1/4" diameter drag washer (x1)
4. Penn 20T & 30S- 2 3/4" diameter drag washers (x1)
5. Penn 16S- 2 1/2" diameter drag washer (x1)
6. Penn 12LT- 1" diameter drag washer (x1)
7. Penn Senator 112H 3/O H- 1" drag washer (x2)
8. Daiwa Sealine 6/O- 1 3/16" drag washer (x3)

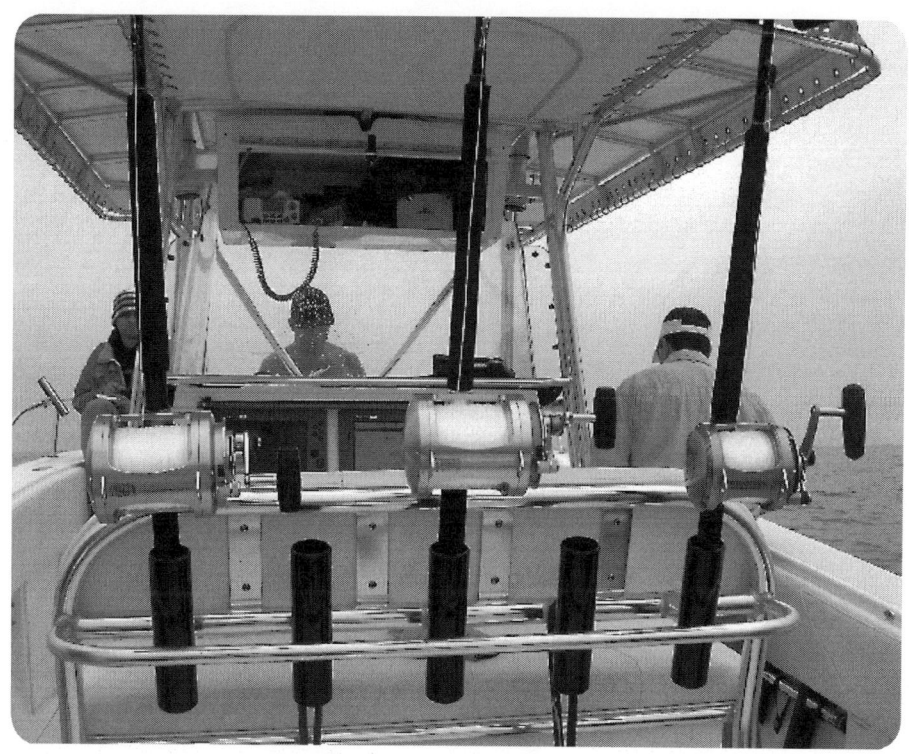

RECOMMENDED RODS AND REELS

The rods and reels I use and recommend for shark fishing along with configurations and reasons are listed on the next few pages. You won't need all of these configurations, just one with which you are comfortable and that you want to use. You don't need the biggest and most expensive equipment, so consider your options before making a purchase. For example, do you want to fish light or heavy? Can you chase a fish or not? For example, using the first setup below (Penn 16S 2 speed), I am able to catch and release large Makos with the ease and enjoyment of using ultra-light tackle. The catch and release did take four hours, but it was all stand-up gear without a harness, and that's what dreams are made of for the big ones.

After these set-ups, there is a detailed explanation (along with grouping and categorization) which explains the purposes of each setup.

1. **Setup (Shotgun rig)**
    a. Rod: Custom Calstar 700M 20-50 pound graphite
        i. Fuji SIC/USG guides
    b. Reel: Penn 16S 2 Speed
        i. Specially modified bearings with Tiburon topless international series custom frame kit, for ease of casting and thumbing the spool.
    c. Line: 50 pound Spectra and 100 pound Top-Shot (100 yards of Momoi Hi-Catch mono)
    d. Leader: See 4, 5, 6, 10 on "rig setups" chart (Chapter Rigging Leaders page 66).

2. **Setup (Shotgun rig)**
    a. Rod: Custom Calstar graphite 700XL 30-80 pound graphite
        i. Fuji SIC/USG guides.
    b. Reel: Penn 16S 2 Speed
        i. Specially modified bearings with Tiburon topless international series custom frame kit, for ease of casting and thumbing the spool.
    c. Line: 50 pound Spectra and 100 pound Top-Shot (100 yards of Momoi Hi-Catch mono)
    d. Leader: See 4, 5, 6, 10 on "rig setups" chart (Chapter Rigging Leaders page 66).

3. **Setup (Shotgun rig)**
    a. Rod: Custom Calstar 760M 40-100 pound
        i. Fuji SIC/USG guides
    b. Reel: Penn International V 50VSW
    c. Line: Mono IGFA 80 pound
    d. Leader: See (1, 2, 3, 9) or (7, 8) on "rig setups" chart (Chapter Rigging Leaders page 66)

4. **Setup (Trolling or drift bait)**
    a. Rod: Black Steel, Seeker G6460XH-6AR 40-100 pound
    b. Reel: Penn Reels 50SW
    c. Line: Mono IGFA 80 pound
    d. Leader: See 7, 8, 11, 12, 13 on "rig setups" chart (Chapter Rigging Leaders page 66)

5. **Setup (Trolling or drift bait)**
    a. Rod: Black Steel, Seeker G6460XH-6AR 40-100 pound
    b. Reel: Penn Reels 50SW
    c. Line: Mono IGFA 80 pound
    d. Leader: See 7, 8, 11, 12, 13 on "rig setups" chart (Chapter Rigging Leaders page 66)

6. **Setup (Drift bait)**
    a. Rod: Black Steel, Seeker G6463XXH-6 ¼ AR 60(80)100
    b. Reel: Penn International 70 Big game special
    c. Line: Mono IGFA 80 pound
    d. Leader: See 11, 12, 13 on "rig setups" chart (Chapter Rigging Leaders page 86)

7. **Setup (Drift bait)**
    a. Rod: Black Steel, Seeker G643XXH-6 ¼ AR 50(80)130 pound
    b. Reel: Shimano Tiagra 80W
    c. Line: Mono IGFA 80 pound
    d. Leader: See 11, 12, 13 on "rig setups" chart (Chapter Rigging Leaders page 66)

8. **Setup (Drift bait)**
    a. Rod: Black Steel, Seeker G643XXH-6 ¼ AR 50(80)130 pound
    b. Reel: Shimano Tiagra 80W
    c. Line: Mono IGFA 80 or 130 pound
    d. Leader: See 11, 12, 13 on "rig setups" chart (Chapter Rigging Leaders page 66)

BIG FISH SETUPS 6, 7, 8

Leaders, I use #16 or #17 for the 500lb fish and up! The 25' of cable will come in handy when its time to leader the fish.
I use to use spectra line for banking on my 50-80s, but now I find it cheaper and easier to maintain and wash down the reels without worrying that the spectra will rot.

OPTIONAL, FOR TAGGING AND FIGHTING SMALLER SHARKS (ULTRA-LIGHT DIVISION) OR ELIGIBILITY FOR IGFA WORLD RECORDS:

9. **Setup (100 pound and under)**
    a. Rod: Custom Calstar Graphite 700XL 10-25 pound
        i. Fuji SIC/USG guide
    b. Reel: Shimano Trinidad TN14
    c. Line: 8 pound test IGFA GRN
    d. Leader: See (1, 2, 3) or (8) on "rig setups" chart for strand type (Chapter Rigging Leaders page 66). Use any length up to 30 feet.

10. **Setup (100 pound and under)**
    a. Rod: Custom Calstar Graphite 700L 15-30 pound
        i. Fuji SIC/USG guide
    b. Reel: Shimano Trinidad TN16
    c. Line: 12 pound test IGFA GRN
    d. Leader: See (1, 2, 3) or (8, 11) on "rig setups" chart for strand type (Chapter Rigging Leaders page 66). Use any length up to 30 feet.

11. **Setup (100 pound and under)**
    a. Rod: Custom Calstar Graphite 700L 15-30 pound
        i. Fuji SIC/USG guide
    b. Reel: Shimano Trinidad TN20
    c. Line: 20 pound test IGFA GRN
    d. Leader: See (1, 2, 3) or (8, 11, 12) on "rig setups" chart for strand type (Chapter Rigging Leaders page 66). Use any length up to 30 feet.

12. **Setup (100 pound and under)**
    a. Rod: Custom Calstar Graphite 700M 20-50 pound
        i. Fuji SIC/USG guide
    b. Reel: Shimano Trinidad TN30
    c. Line: 30 pound test IGFA GRN
    d. See (1, 2, 3) or (8, 11, 12, 13) on "rig setups" chart for strand type (Chapter Rigging Leaders page 66). Use any length up to 30 feet.

13. **Setup (Trolling)**
    a. Rod: Seeker SC660XH-6' RS/RT 40(50)100 pound
    b. Reel: Shimano TLD 2 SPEED 30
    c. Line: 50 pound Mono
    d. Leader: 15 ft stranded leader (150–400 pound), or lure with 15 ft stranded leader (150 – 400 pound).

14. **Setup (Trolling)**
    a. Rod: Seeker SC660XH-6' RS/RT 40(50)100 pounds
    b. Reel: Shimano TLD 2 SPEED 30
    c. Line: 50 pound Ande Mono
    d. Leader: 15 ft stranded leader (150–400 pound), or lure with 15 ft stranded leader (150–400 pound).

15. **Setup (Trolling)**
    a. Rod: Black Steel, Seeker graphite G6460H-6' RS/RT 40(50)60 pound
    b. Reel: Shimano Triton Beast Master 30/50 Two Speed
    c. Line: 60 pound
    d. Leader: 15 ft stranded leader (150 – 400 pound), or lure with 15 ft stranded leader (150 – 400 pound).

For Bait Rigs Only:

16. **Setup (Bait rod)**
    a. Rod: Penn Special
    b. Reel: Penn Levelwind
    c. Line: 20 pound test Ande Mono
    d. Sabiki or Yo-zuri bait rigs.

These rods and reels have been placed in groups (below) to better explain their purposes and to categorize them for particular events. Look over each group carefully to see if you currently have anything similar to the listed setups. If you are not sure, you may be able to simply change the line weight to fit that rod and reel into the appropriate category.

Rod and reel setup #12 should be used for each group, and left on the boat so you always have access to it. You need at least one bait rod.

Group 1 - Throwing Bait……………………….. (1, 2, 3)

Shotgun rigged for lightweight (1, 2) and heavyweight (3) tackle. Lightweight shotgun rigs are great for tossing live or dead bait to the fish. Heavyweight shotgun rigs are ideal for bigger fish that swim right to the boat. These give you the flexibility to drop or cast a bait right in front of the shark.

Group 2 - Trolling or Drift Bait………………. (4, 5)

Specialized in trolling for larger sharks and drift baiting. It is also a more affordable and likely alternative to group 3.

Group 3 - Drift Bait……………………………. (6, 7, 8)

This group uses some of the best quality reels on the market, which I use solely for drift baiting. These are your big guns and are best suited to handle the largest sharks in the ocean, and also have the largest line capacity.

Using this three set combination, each rod serves its own purpose. I put #9 right at the boat, #10 about 20-30 yards out, and #11 from 25-35 yards out. For setup #9, I like to use leader #11 (according to the rig setups chart) because it allows me to utilize small bait.

For setup #10, I use leader #12 because it allows me to utilize medium sized bait. Last, for setup #11, I like to use leader #13 because it allows me to utilize large bait.

While you can rig these for trolling, I advise against doing so because you may get a fray or twist in your line and not know it. Then the next time you use your rod and reel to hook into a large Mako, the line will start screaming off the reel. As you see or feel the fray zooming past the rod tip, you will realize that your chances of catching this beast have greatly diminished. Trying to recover the frayed line as quickly as possible is a compromised position in which to be, as getting to the recovery point may take a long period of time. When you are fishing for sea monsters, you want your line in the best shape as possible.

Group 4 - The 100 Pound and Under Catches…(9, 10, 11, 12)

The National Marine Fisheries' Shark Tagging Program states that the average weight of a tagged and released shark is just less than 100 pounds. Most of my tag and releases are less than 100 pounds. You will want a rig specifically set up for catching smaller Makos. Some of my most enjoyable shark fishing experiences entailed fighting small Makos with light tackle. I've noticed that when I'm using lighter tackle, Makos can become very acrobatic. Watching them "put on a show" for you is an experience in itself.

By having these rods on board and ready to use, when a small Mako swims up the slick, I quickly grab the appropriate rod and bait it, ready to catch these scaled-down monsters. In these situations, one of the things I love most to do is hand the baited rod to a guest (first time fisherman, or experienced fisherman who is skeptical about shark fishing) and tell him where to cast it in order to get the fish to bite. Once he hooks the fish, he hooks himself on shark fishing.

Group 5 - Trolling……………………………… (13, 14, 15)

This is an ideal setup for trolling small Makos and threshers, due to the durability, non-scratch surface, and line capacity. Setups 1 and 2 are for surface and deep diving rules. Setup #3 is for the down rigger.

Bait Rod……………………………………... (16)

Put on a four- to six-ounce chrome diamond jig. You can put pieces of bait on the hook to catch mackerel, or troll slowly to catch mackerel and bonitoes.

Alternative Grouping

While I recommend grouping your rods and reels as listed above, you can customize your setup to an extent. For example, you might have 4, 5, 6, and one rod and reel from group 1 grouped together, a nice set.

Tournament Grouping

For grouping the rods and reels for big catch, and catch and release tournaments, see the section on tournaments.

Drag Scale Settings

While you may think you can suffice without one, I recommend you don't go fishing without a quality scale. Fishing for halibut is one thing, but when a 300+ pound Mako is on the line, if you don't have the proper drag settings you're going to be in trouble.

Drag Settings for your Line
130lb line: 35-40 pounds of strike drag.
80lb line: 25-30 pounds of strike drag.
50lb line: 10-15 pounds of strike drag
30lb line: 10 pounds of strike drag.
20lb line: 5 pounds of strike drag.
Lighter line: 25-30% of the breaking strength

Be sure to get a drag scale with a slide marker. To use it, have one guy hold the scale (with the line tied to it), while the other guy lifts the rod until the line comes off the reel at the right drag pressure. Make adjustments if necessary. When a Mako makes a fast run, you may need to back off on the drag pressure a bit. If you can't get the shark up from the depths or to the boat, you may need to increase your reel drag pressure to full or better than 60% of the breaking strength of the line. This can be tricky, and should only be done by someone who knows what he or she is doing with the gear and the sharks characteristics.

For more information on how to set your drags, there are books and videos you can purchase online or at your local tackle shop.

My rule of thumb is to set the drag to 1/3 of the breaking strength of the line.

Customizing Reels
For many Shimano and Penn reels, there is a very nice replacement bearing kit you can get installed, called Cal's Special Bearing Kit. These are lube-plated, high precision, high performance, free spool bearings; they are incredibly useful for bait casting. Though the manufacturer claims these bearings increase spool rotations generally 2 to 3 times longer than stock bearings, he's being very modest.

In addition to replacing the bearings, you can add on a sleeve. The sleeve increases spool rotation an additional 50%, on top of the increase from the bearings. The installation is done on the outside diameter of the drag and increases the drag average radius in addition to the drag area itself. This will give you over 100% more drag at the same preset, meaning you can back your preset off to get the same amount of drag with which you are already fishing. By using this larger drag, the internal load on the real is drastically reduced. I have gotten this done to both of my Penn 16S reels, and highly recommend it to everyone. For more information on Cal's bearing kits, visit their website at *www.cals2speed.com*.

Safety

- On big game or trolling rods, always use a safety strap.
- Make sure the lines on your reels do not get damaged while stowed or traveling, as damage may cause a nick or fray in the line.
- Recheck the reel mounting screws often, as vibrations from the boat may loosen them.
- Don't get your thumb caught in the spool as a fish is running.
- If a fish is running, be careful when you finger the line, as it will burn you.
- Be careful to not let a baited or hooked line get wrapped around any part of your body.

Maintenance

- Though reels may come with reel covers upon purchase, I strongly recommend purchasing a better one.
- Clean your rods and reels after every use with fresh water, Saltex and WD-40. Do NOT soak Dacron or Spectra lines with water on your reel.
- Keep covers on your rods and reels when they are not being used.
- Replace line when necessary, which is typically after about a year or after a big fish has been caught. I replace my line (mono) every year or as needed. Dacron can last for a few years before needing to be replaced.
- On Dacron lines, strip off and remove 50 feet before every use, as the sun bakes the wax right off the line, making the line brittle and weak.
- Mono line, always check for nicks or frays on your line as you let it out. If you find any, promptly remove that section of the line.

Keeping your gear top notch and always maintained, you will be ready for the big one!

Belts and Harnesses

Most boats on the East Coast are equipped with fighting chairs. Most boats on the West Coast are equipped with bait tanks instead. To fish for Makos, you need a butt belt and a fighting harness. Fishing for Makos is nothing like fishing for marlin—when compared to Makos, marlin are carps.

The Mad Minute
On one fishing trip I got a good hook set on a roughly 800 pound Mako that was cruising about 50 yards behind the boat. I must have hurt it when setting the hook because it went ballistic. It raced toward the stern of the boat at an incredibly fast speed. As I was trying to reel in the slack, the fish went airborne 20 yards off the starboard side, heading straight toward the bow. I ran up to the bow, and the fish sounded, taking 200 yards of line toward the port side. As I was approaching port side, the Mako leaped 20 yards off the stern, instead of sounding as I had originally thought. I immediately went back to the stern and continued fighting the fish. This was the most hectic 30 seconds of my life. Had I been in a fighting chair while this happened, the line would have been sawed off somewhere on the hull of the boat.

Using a fighting belt gives you great maneuverability and better leverage on heavy fish by putting the force on your back and arms. A belt coupled with a harness distributes the force between your legs and buttocks in addition to your back and arms.

Butt (Gimbal) Belt

Butt belts are designed for resting the butt of the rod in a cup, commonly known as a gimbal, allowing the rod to pivot as you pull up and reel down. I use a Braid brand butt belt. Braid belts are simple to use, and can be put on quickly. A typical shark battle requires only a butt belt, but if you're dealing with large Mako, it is best to use a fighting harness as well.

Fighting Belt

Fighting belts are used when a butt belt won't suffice. The Braid Power Play belt is a good choice. The Braid Power Play comes with extra padding for your legs that is helpful for enduring long fights.

Fighting Harness

When a fighting belt just isn't enough, you can accompany it with a fighting harness. You need this gear for stand up fighting. I use a Braid Power Play fighting harness. Quality built, with back and seat support keeps you on top of the big fish and the stainless "D" rings accommodate drop straps for your fighting belt. The drop straps are for adding additional extensions, connecting from the "D" rings to your fishing reel itself.

Safety
- Butt (leather gimbal) belt
    - Be careful when fighting a fish from the butt belt as you are making your way around the bow of the boat. On some boats, the walk-around is too small to fight a large fish with a butt belt on.
    - Be careful to not let your fishing rod twist.
    - Rods pop out of the gimbal at the most inopportune times; be prepared for this to happen.
    - Keep an eye on the Velcro strap while fighting a fish, as it may loosen or become undone.

- Fighting belt
    - A quick release safety kit is a helpful option.

- Fighting harness (in addition to the above tips)
    - The safest way to equip a fighting harness is to strap it *only* to the fighting belt.
    - If you have added additional straps to the harness that connects to the reel, you must remember that you are physically connected to the fish. In the event that a fish pulls you overboard, your chances of surviving are much higher if you have a quick release function on your harness.

Boat Tools and Fishing Equipment

Over the years of big game fishing, I've used various tools and equipment. I started off using whatever household gear I could gather and store on my boat. The quality of these tools and equipment was lacking. Not only do you need to obtain quality tools and equipment, but you need to care for them properly as well. You don't want to rely on a generic crimping tool and find that when you need it, it's rusted shut. All the tools and equipment in this list have proven beneficial or necessary during the numerous trials of my offshore fishing experiences. As quality increases, so does the price, but higher quality tools last longer and make life a whole lot easier.

Binoculars

A good set of binoculars makes the difference of spotting and identifying fish. When you hunt, you want the meanest set you can get your hands on. This is definitely one of the most important hunting tools you can get. You might also consider stabilizer binoculars.

I recommend Tasco offshore OS541 binoculars. They feature 7X magnification, a wide field of view (366 ft/122 m - at 1000 yards/meters), rubicon-coated objective lenses, and a built-in compass. They are waterproof, easy to focus, and have high clarity.

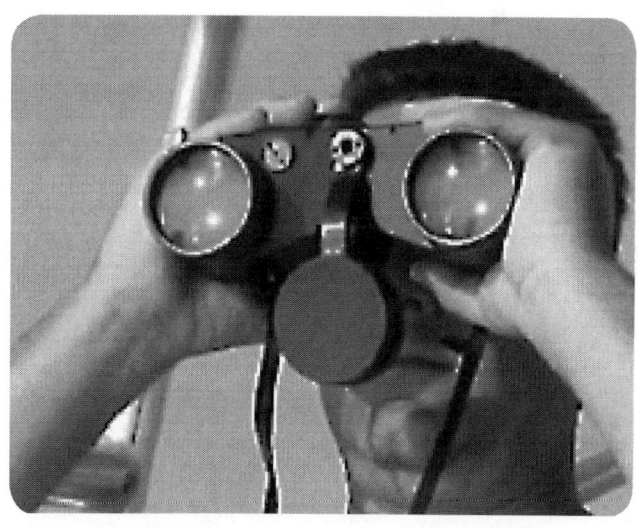

Tasco offshore OS541 binoculars

Wiring Gloves

Leather gloves are a must when wiring a fish. I recommend Campbell Hausfeld welding gloves. I like these because they are thick, padded, and go higher up on your arms than a pair of normal gloves. I feel like I am wearing body armor when wearing these gloves.

Cambell Hausfeld welding gloves

Cutting and Crimping Tools

These are my recommended tools for cutting and crimping. It is important to choose high-quality crimpers and cutters because when you need them, they have to perform well.

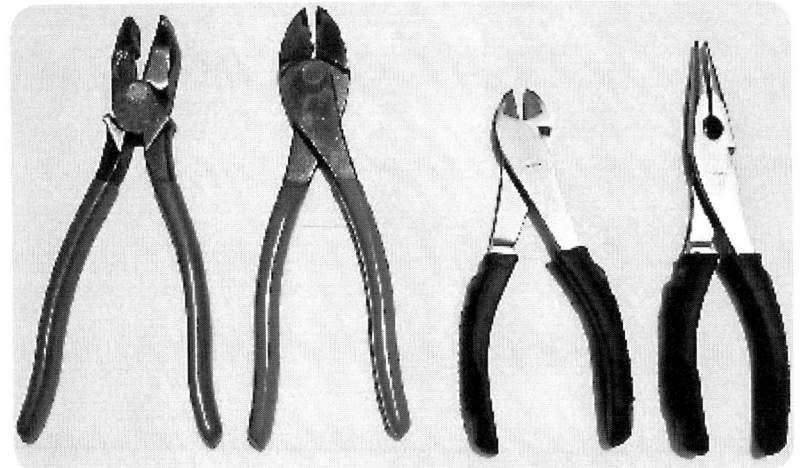

Pictured from left to right:
- *Klein Tools, D2000-9NE side cutting pliers (nines)*
- *Mason crimping tool with wire cutter, extra heavy duty, designed for crimping sleeves size A1 - A10*
- *Shimano Titanium coated diagonal cutting pliers with rubber handles*
- *Shimano Titanium coated needle nose pliers with cutter and rubber handles*

Another good option is a heavy duty, industrial grade, spring loaded crimper. They require less pressure for crimping due to their springs. I prefer these crimping tools as they are the easiest to use.

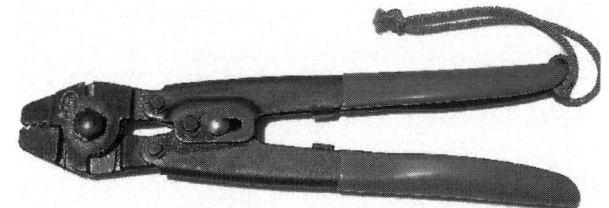

Industrial grade, Spring-loaded crimper for 800 lbs or under

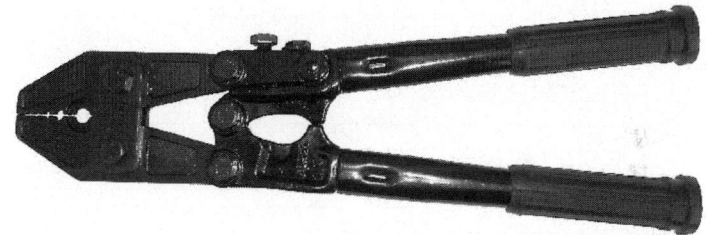

Heavy duty hand crimper CH-18 for 800 lbs and up

Chemical Resistant Gloves

I strongly suggest getting a pair of chemical resistant gloves, as regular gloves will not protect you from tainted bait. I recommend Stanley Chemical Resistant Gloves. They are great for handling chum, and easy to slip on and off.

Bolt Cutters

Bolt cutters are used for cutting hooks out of the jaws of a shark. They are also good for cutting a hook if it gets caught on you or a mate! I recommend the Toolsmith Bolt Cutter.

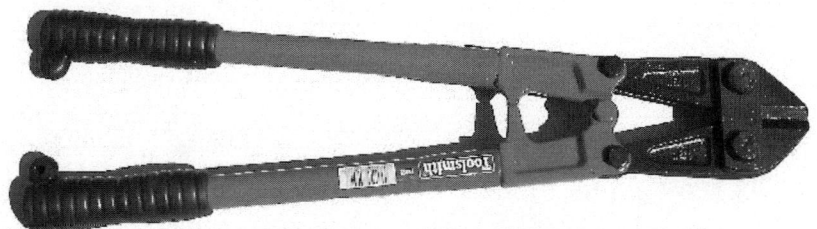

Toolsmith Bolt Cutter

Bait Needle
You can purchase these fairly cheaply. They are necessary for rigging bait.

6" Bait needle

Steel Hook File
You will need a 5½" high carbon, steel hook file with an ultra-fine cutting edge.

Serrated Buck Knife
You will need a serrated Buck knife with 2½" skinning blade. These make a great safety backup tool for quickly cutting line or rope.

Industrial Hanging Scale
A heavy duty hanging scale is ideal for weighing Makos. They are especially helpful for seeing if your catch is a qualifying fish for tournaments. A scale that measures up to 300 pounds is adequate.

Maps
You will need local and offshore maps. Up-to-date temperature, wind vector and tide charts are a must to have on board.

Normark K-Steel Fillet Glove
These helpful gloves combine "new twist" yarn with steel flex fibers. They resist cuts from fillet knives, fit either hand, and are machine washable.

Cutting Board
I recommend the Fentress Rigging and Bait Tray. It folds flat for storage and has stainless steel fasteners.

Mag-lite

I've gone through many waterproof flashlights and cheap, plastic flashlights. They failed when I needed them. The Mag-lite is a heavy-duty, water-resistant, steel flashlight with three-plus batteries. They always include a spare bulb. This flashlight is very reliable, unlike standard flashlights.

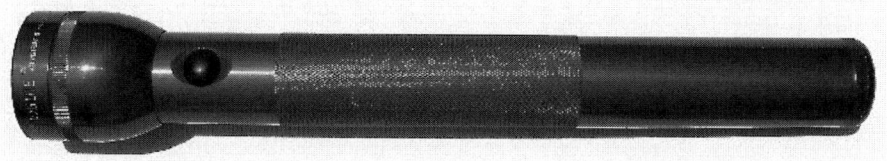

2 Million Candle Power High Beam Light

You will find a high-quality two-million candle power, high beam light a useful tool to have onboard. It is specifically used for night fishing, and for signaling in an emergency, though you are sure to find a couple dozen other uses for this tool.

100 lb Scale

This scale has a slide maker that makes it easy to set drag pressure on your reels.

Low Voltage Circuit Tester, Digital Multi-Meter/Ohm Meter

Your whole boat's function is based around your battery power. You will need to know if your battery is working properly. These tools will alleviate guesswork when you're out on the ocean.

Spare Spark Plugs, Socket, and Ratchet

Sometimes the simplest things are often overlooked. If your motor fouls a plug, you will want to be able to fix this very common problem.

Eyewear, Sunscreen, Hat

These items are critical to protect you from the harmful rays of the sun. Choose polarized glasses because the polarization allows you to see fish below the surface.

Small Butane Torch, Solder, and Electrical Wire

These items are needed for electrical repairs.

Deck of Cards

Hey, things get slow on the grounds, and what better way to pass the time than playing some five card draw?

ELECTRONIC ATTRACTING DEVICES

As you know, shark fishing isn't cheap. You have invested an untold amount on your boat and in equipment, rods, reels, and gaffs. After spending all this money, you probably think you're all set and ready to go, but if you're really serious about catching the beasts and winning tournaments, there's one thing left to get: an electronic attractant. Though the device itself is fairly expensive, it pays for itself very quickly. When you consider how much you spend on gas and chum, you don't want to come home empty-handed. This device attracts Mako sharks. Each time I use an electronic attractant, more fish are attracted to the boat. When I don't use this device, I often see monster sharks swim through the slick and leave. They will eat the bait that was eating your chum 50 yards behind the boat, without approaching your boat.

The Sonic

The Sonic imitates the sound frequencies that a wounded bait fish would produce, which attracts sharks. The Sonic gives off this low frequency tone of acoustic vibrations in a 360 degree pattern, inviting sharks to the boat. The Sonic can be heard for at least one mile through the water. While chum is only spread in one direction, this device rings the dinner bell in all directions.

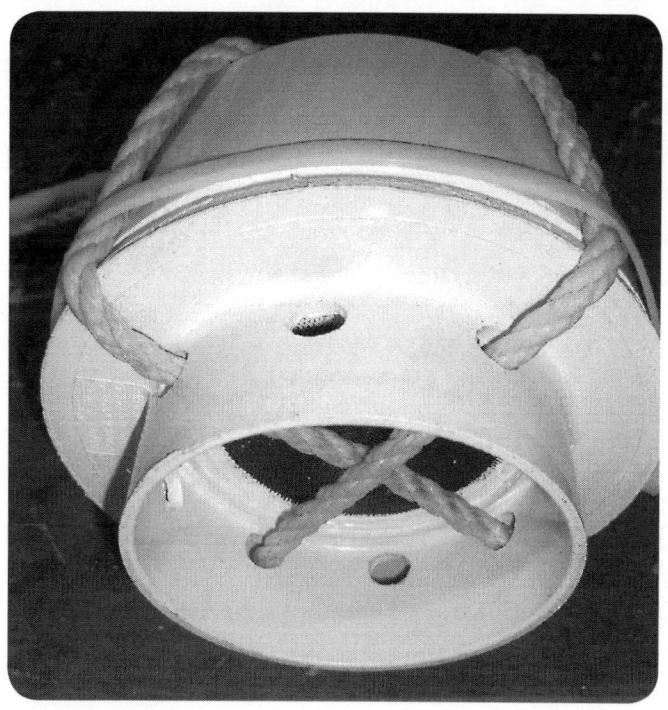

Typically a shark approaches the boat because the chum slick has attracted it. Most of the time it doesn't head straight for the chum bucket. Sharks have bio-electrical sensors called *ampullae of Lorenzini*, (see *The Mako Shark*) which help sharks find low frequency electrical currents emitted by fish. Because of the many electrical currents generated by your boat, (the grounding system tied in with the motor and zincs) the shark usually heads for the propeller, which protrudes from the boat giving off an electrical current. (This is why some sharks bite into the propeller). The next thing sharks tend to investigate is the chum bucket. The Sonic is such a strong attractant that sharks will bypass the propeller, the zincs, and the chum bucket to head straight for the Sonic.

LINE, HOOKS & RIGGING LEADERS

When rigging leaders, lines and hooks you should use the best quality and brand names you can get. You should also use simple, uncomplicated connections; the simpler it is, the less probability that things will go wrong. Since monster Makos can bite through wire leaders, I recommend 800 pound, 30 foot leaders for the big ones.

You're big game hunting now, not fishing at your local lake. Think of trying to hold onto a 1000 pound tiger—what type of connection would you want, one that is complicated and weak or one that is simple and strong?

Lines

There are three types of line you will be using: Dacron, mono, and spectra. Each line has its pros and cons. For world records, you must use IGFA certified line. Most tournaments don't allow you to exceed the 130 pound IGFA class line.

Mono line (made of extruded nylon) is slightly thicker than Dacron. An 80 pound test mono line will be thicker than an 80 pound test Dacron. Mono line is also fairly stiff and consists of only a single filament (monofilament), while Dacron line has multiple braided filaments. Since the fibers on a Dacron line are so tightly braided, it has no stretch; mono line has a little bit of stretch. Mono line is thicker than Dacron, so you can't hold as much on a reel. Since mono line tends to stretch, it is harder to set the hook.

Every time you use Dacron line that has had previous use, you should spool and cut off 50 feet of the line. The sun's UV rays melt wax off the line while it is in the water, which dries out the line, deteriorating and weakening it. The slightest loss of line strength makes all the difference in the world. If you see or feel a nick or fray in the line, cut off that part of the line, whether it's 10 feet or 100 feet.

Spectra line is a higher grade, expensive version of Dacron lines. It is sturdier, smaller in diameter, and used mainly for backing. It has a Polymer Reinforced Technology (PRT) coating which allows you to use a broader range of knots; the coating provides a better grip and prevents knot slippage.

Other than personal preference and knot tying ability, neither line is better than the other. Since mono line is made of nylon, when it gets wet, it quickly dries off. Since Dacron line is so tightly braided, if any water sinks into it, it will rot the line from the inside. I've even seen reels that deteriorated underneath wet areas on Dacron line.

This is an example of a rotted Dacron line. Instead of a bone white color, the line has rotted into a dirty golden-brown, due to poor maintenance

Recommended Knots
Mono: Double Shark Knot
Dacron: Cats Paw

Wire Leaders

Single Strand Wire
For all of the following, use Either Berkley Big Game stainless steel or Single Strand chrome nickel alloy.

1. 120 lb, .024 diameter, 25 ft
2. 174 lb, .029 diameter, 25 ft
3. 240 lb, .035 diameter, 25 ft
4. 360 lb, .043 diameter, 25 ft
5. 400 lb, .045 diameter, 25 ft

Stranded Wire

All the following are Duratest and or Malin 49 Stranded Stainless Steel Cable.

1. 150 lb 49 Strand, A4 sleeve, Mason 21D 90-210 lb double connector sleeves
2. 400 lb 49 Strand, A8 sleeve, Mason 41D 210-480 lb double connector sleeves
3. 600 lb 49 Strand, A9 sleeve, Mason 51D 600 lb double connector sleeves
4. 800 lb 49 Strand, A12 sleeve, Mason 61D 800 lb double connector sleeves Malin 49 Strand Stainless Steel Cable
5. 920 lb 49 Strand, MIT Compression Swages PM5 (.094) Diameter in inches.

Single strand wires have a very high strength to diameter ratio for use as leader material. They should be used for smaller Makos and shotgun rigs. Stranded wires are more flexible and durable, making them adequate for larger Makos. Always have on your boat a 30' 920 lb wire leader with a 14/0 on it ready for action. And have a 3' 240 lb single strand shotgun rig with a 7/0 on it ready to go!

Hooks

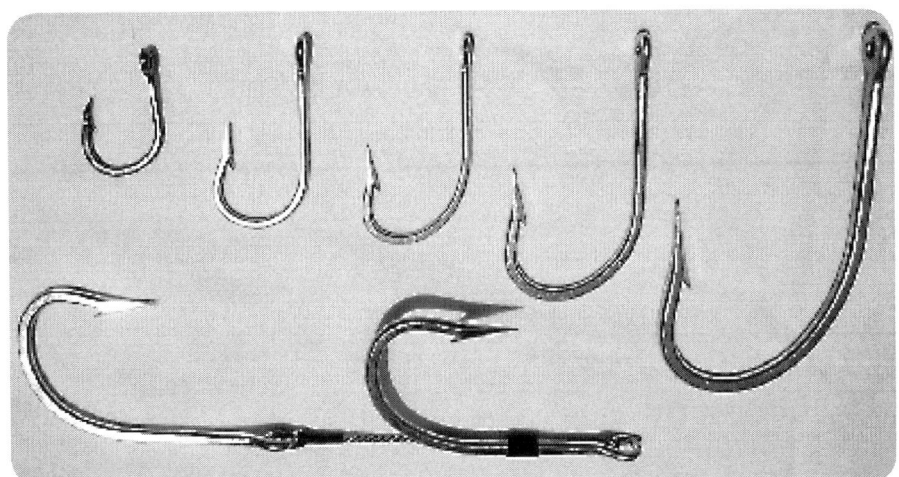

Hooks for Dead Bait

Owner hooks do not require sharpening, while the rest do. I always give my Mustad hooks (the ones listed below) a needle-point edge and never use them standard out of the box.

1. Mustad Ref/Part #7691S (Southern & Tuna-forged, knife edge point, ringed, stainless steel)
    a. 7/0 non-welded eye
    b. I can get a sharper edge on stainless steel hooks, making them easy to bury into a fish for a quick catch and release.

2. Mustad Ref/Part #7731(Sea Demon-forged, knife edge point, ringed)
    a. 7/0 welded eye
    b. 10/0 welded eye
    c. 12/0 welded eye
    d. 14/0 welded eye
        I like this particular model because it is open hook (the shank points straight out), and not curved in like most live bait hooks.

3. Allen Comstock Ultra Pro Rig, Ref/Part # UP14 7731
    a. 11/0 welded eye, double hooked
        Used for trolling lures by them, with live bait, or with cut bait.

Live Bait Hooks

Owner hooks do not require sharpening, while the rest do.

1. Owner Ref/Part #5105R-151 (Cutting point, ringed gorilla style. Outside forging, triple edged cutting blade.)
    a. 5/0 non-welded eye
    b. Recommended for small mackerel and large sardines or herrings, for thresher fishing
    c. Allows bait to swim freely for live bait fishing, while the leader is tied to the ring, and not the hook.

2. Owner Ref/Part #5305-171 (Cutting point, gorilla style. Outside forging, triple edged cutting blade.)
   a. 7/0 non-welded eye
   Recommended for small mackerel

3. Mustad ref/part #7691S (Southern & Tuna-forged, knife edge point, stainless steel)
   a. 7/0 non-welded eye
   b. Recommended for small and large mackerel
   c. Curved in hook keeps live bait on the hook well.

Sharpening Hooks

For your own safety, don't sharpen your hook until you're absolutely ready to use it. Keep your leader off the deck while you're sharpening your hook. Someone could get a foot tangled in it or pull on it, putting the hook straight into your hand.

Procedure for Sharpening Hooks

Hold the sharpening stone with one hand and the hook with the other hand. The proper way to sharpen a hook is to strike in the direction that the tip of the hook is pointed. For example, in the picture above, you would run the hook downward, because the tip of the hook is facing down. Sharpen the hook on the two flat sides and the side of the tip facing out. Sharpen until you achieve a fine, needle point.

Rig Setups Chart

To determine the hook type, check if the bait is live or dead and compare with the previous list.

	Bait	Hook size	Hook type	Single strand	Multi-strand	Rig type	Length	Fish size
1	Live	5/0	Owner nwe	150 lb			6 ft	Small
2	Live	7/0	Owner nwe	174 lb			12 ft	Small
3	Live	7/0	Mustad nwe	240 lb			8 ft	Medium
4	Dead	7/0	Mustad fwe	140 lb		Shotgun	3 ft	Small
5	Dead	7/0	Mustad fwe	240 lb		Shotgun	3 ft	Medium
6	Dead	7/0	Mustad fwe	400 lb		Shotgun	3 ft	Large
7	Dead	7/0	Mustad fwe		150 lb		15 ft	Small
8	Live	7/0	Mustad nwe		150 lb		15 ft	Small
9	Both	7/0	Mustad nwe	240 lb			8 ft	Medium
10	Dead	10/0	Mustad fwe	400 lb		Shotgun	4 ft	Large
11	Dead	10/0	Mustad fwe		600 lb		20 ft	Large
12	Dead	12/0	Mustad fwe		800 lb		25 ft	Large
13	Dead	14/0	Mustad fwe		920 lb		30 ft	Large

fwe= forged welded eye / nwe= non-welded eye
All welded eyes are forged, and all non-welded eyes are stainless steel.

Zinc Wire

Twisting a 6 inch piece of zinc wire to your wire leader will create a minute electrical current that could aid in attracting sharks.

WIND-ON LEADERS

Top Shots By Basil

100 yards, 100 lb test mono, and three feet of 130 lb spectra. Momoi Hi-Catch mono, this is the softest line on the market. It is very flexible and casts easily, without sacrificing durability. I prefer to purchase these professionally made wind-on leaders over making them myself.

To order go to, www.bhptackle.com

Completed Rigs

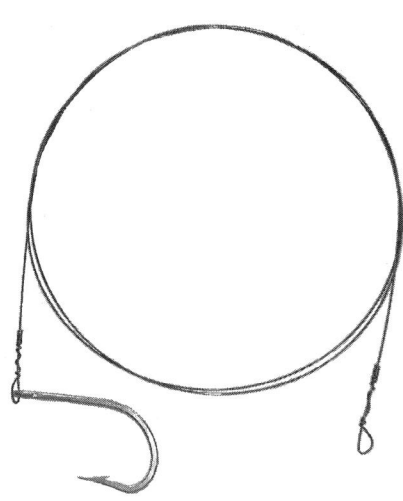

Single strand wire leader

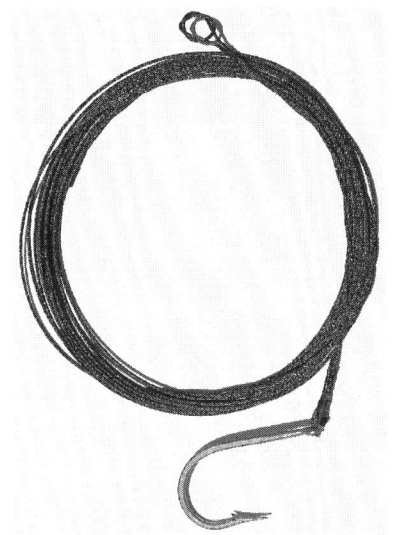

Stranded wire leader

Snap & Ball Bearing Swivels
Aussie swivels-400 lb test
Aussie swivels-600 lb test
Sampo swivels-150 lb test
Sampo swivels-300 lb test
Sampo swivels-500 lb test

Aussie Snap Swivel

Sampo Ball Bearing Snap Swivel

Over the years I have tried just about every combination possible, and this is the best one I have come up with. You can pick up either just a bearing swivel or a bearing and snap swivel. For more information see rigging leaders.

Bait Rigs (used for catching bait)
You can catch bait fish without pieces of bait on the hooks but it is more effective to put bait on the hooks. When baiting a hook, always make sure the hook is exposed.

Sabiki Hayabusa Art #S-002AE, Style HAGE-KAWA (7 lbs branch test, 13 lbs main test, Size 6)
    a. For jigging small bait fish such as sardines and mackerel.
    Sabiki Hayabusa Art #S-501E, Style Mix-yarn (20 lbs branch test, 30 lbs main   test, Size 12).
    b. For jigging small as well as larger bait fish. By adding a diamond jig to the bottom of the rig, you can also slow troll behind the boat and pick up bonitoes.

Before and during construction, make sure your leaders' cuts are clean. I cannot stress enough how important it is to use high quality cutting pliers to prevent frays. The slightest frays will make it tough (or impossible) to pass crimps over your leaders.

When you make any cuts, make sure you grab the end that you are going to cut off. If the wire is firm, you will always get a clean cut, preventing pieces of wire from flying across the room.

> CAUTION: Do not sharpen your hooks until you're out in the water — the moment you are ready to use them.

My tools:
- Klein Tools, D2000-9NE side cutting pliers (nines)
- Mason crimping tool with wire cutter, extra heavy duty
- Shimano titanium-coated diagonal cutting pliers with rubber handles
- Shimano titanium-coated needle nose pliers with cutter and rubber handles
- (Refer to "Tools" section for more information on the crimping tools, pliers and cutters)

You will also need:
- A stranded wire leader of appropriate length
- Keep your length under 30 feet if you want to be eligible for IGFA records.
- Hook and appropriate crimps
- 4 crimps per leader, as you will double-crimp each end)
- Crimp sizes need to match cable size

Double Hook Rig

A double hook can be added to the leader on page 95. Simply rig the second hook to the loop on the hook side. Use the same rigging procedures. Make sure your double hook wire and hook are not longer than the IGFA required length. I would give you the exact measurements but its time for you to log onto *www.igfa.org* and read their rules for yourself.

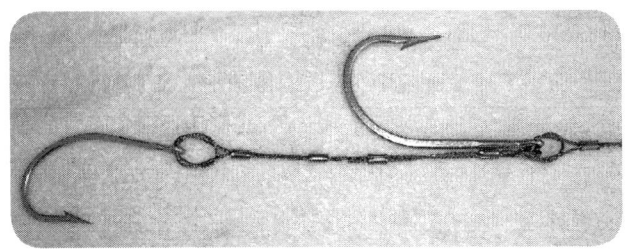

Instructions for Multi Strand Wire Leaders

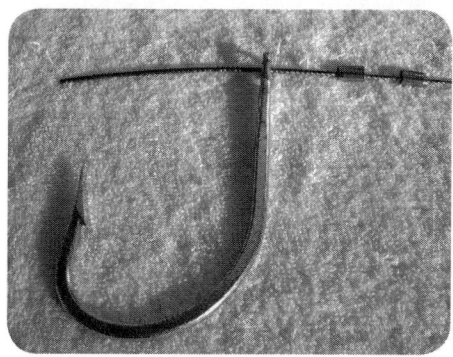

1. Slide two crimps on one end of the leader.
2. Slide your hook down the same end.

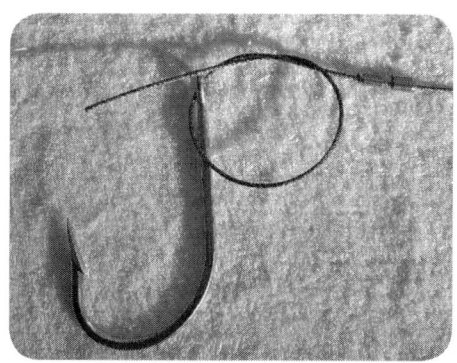

3. Secure the crimps in the palm of your right hand. Grab the wire leader with your right index finger and thumb. Grab tag end with your left hand. With your left hand, make an overhand loop and grab the wire with your right thumb and index finger. The tag end should be in front of the leader side. Tuck the tag end from behind through the already formed loop. The tag end should have approximately 4 inches hanging off of it.

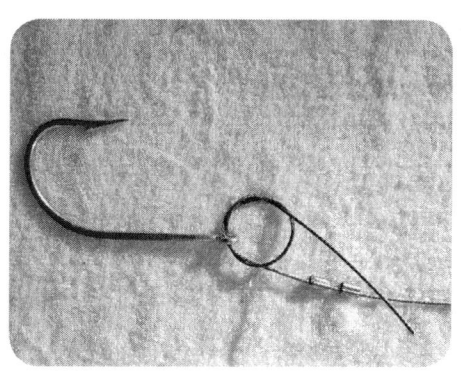

4. Grab the tag end with your left hand. Make a loop by passing the tag end through the back of the loop, and through the eye of the hook.

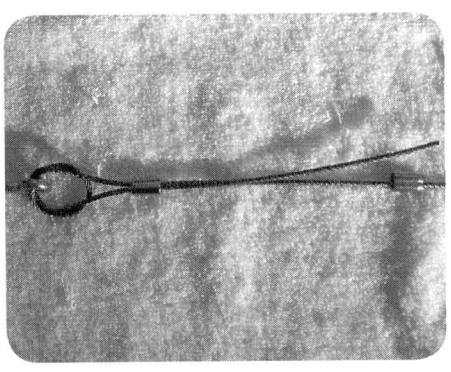

5. Hold the hook firmly in your left hand with your left thumb and index finger on the loop. With your right hand, pull the two ends of the wire; as you pull, work the size of the loop down with your left thumb and index finger, so as not to deform the loop.

6. Pass the first crimp through the tag end.
7. Slide it as close to the loop as possible, and crimp it.

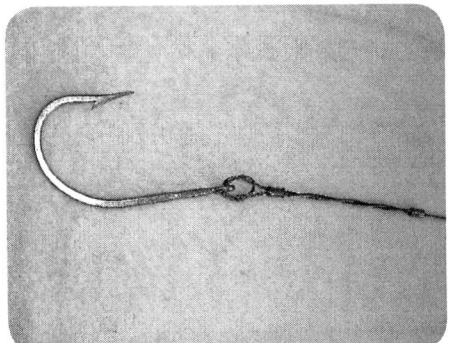

8. Twist the wire leader a few times. Pass the second crimp down over the tag end and crimp it. When you crimp it, be sure to cover the entire wire (on the tag end) and to leave at least a few inches between the crimps.

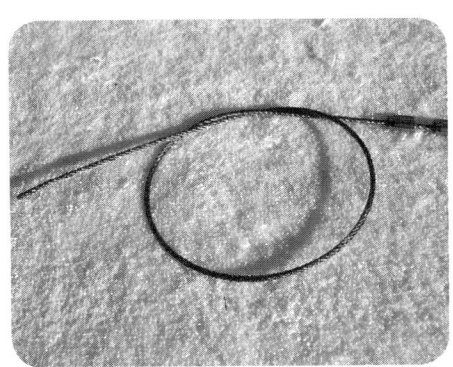

9. Slide two crimps on one end of the leader at about six inches. Secure the crimps in the palm of your right hand. Grab the wire leader with your right index finger and thumb. Grab the tag end with your left hand.

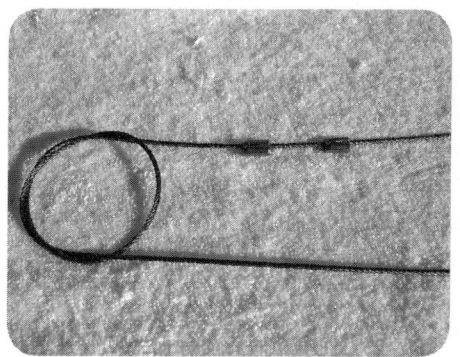

10. With your left hand, make an overhand loop and grab the wire with your right thumb and index finger. The tag end should be in front of the leader side. Tuck the tag end from behind through the already formed loop. Leave at least 3 or 4 inches (or longer) hanging off the tag end.

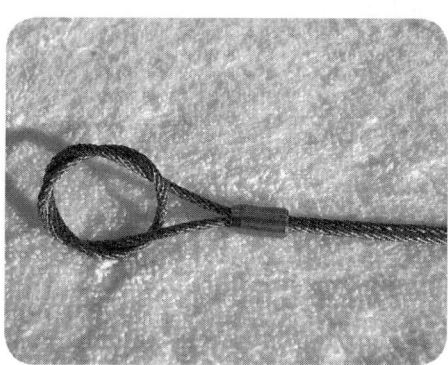

11. Hold the loop with your left thumb and index finger. With your right hand, pull the two ends of the wire, but as you pull work the loop down to a small size with your left thumb and index finger, so as not to deform the loop. Pass the first crimp through the tag end and slide it as close to the loop as possible and crimp it.

12. Twist the wire leader a few times. Pass the second crimp down over the tag end and crimp it. When you crimp it, be sure to cover the entire wire (on the tag end) and to leave at least a few inches between the crimps.

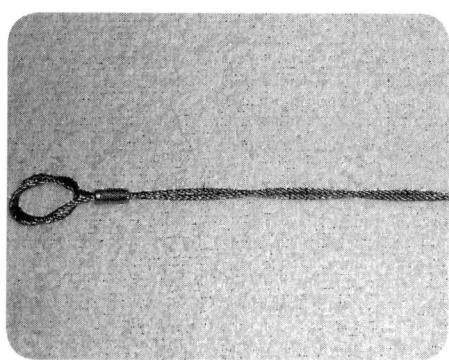

13. You can make the crimp backs as long as you want too. I like to make my last crimp right not the tag end of the wire. Covering the wire strands to protect your hands for when you grab the leader.

A good company to order big game materials from is
www.meltontackle.com.

Haywire Twist (Solid Wire Leaders)

The Haywire Twist is for solid heavy wire, which is used for various length leaders, depending on what you are fishing for, and the size of the fish. These instructions are for just about any size wire, but these photos are of 400 lb single strand wire. On heavy wire wrap the tag end around the main. On less than 180 lb, twist the main and the tag end together.

Procedure:

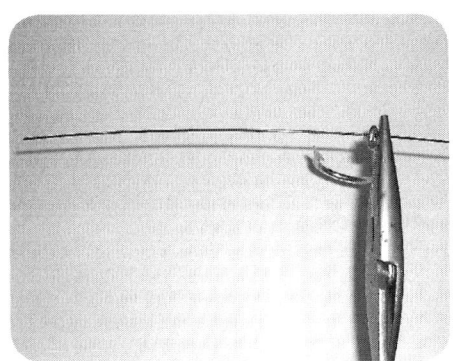

1. With your left hand, grab the wire firmly with a pair of needle nosed pliers. You should have 6-8 inches of wire sticking out on the left (tag) side. Slide your hook over the tag end to the pliers.

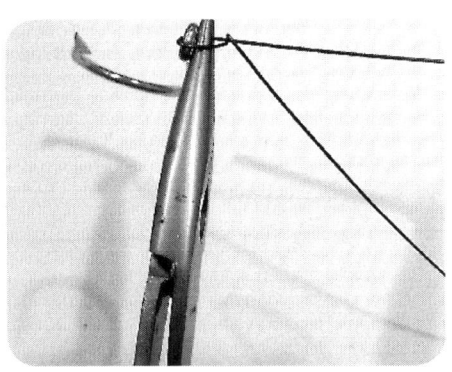

2. Grab the tag end of the wire with your right hand and pull it over the hook and the top of the pliers, and back over on top of the other end of the wire.

3. Push the tag end down with your right thumb, resting on the right side of the pliers. The tag end should be in front of the long end and facing down completely.

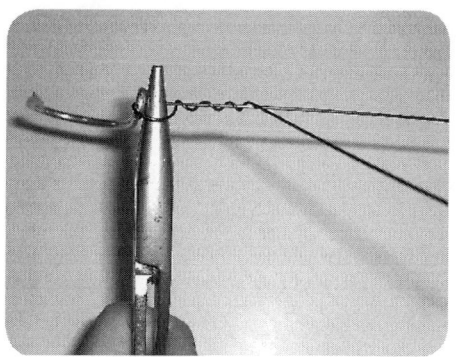

4. With your right hand, bring the tag end down, toward you, and begin to loosely wrap the tag end of the wire around the long end. Make four complete wide wraps.

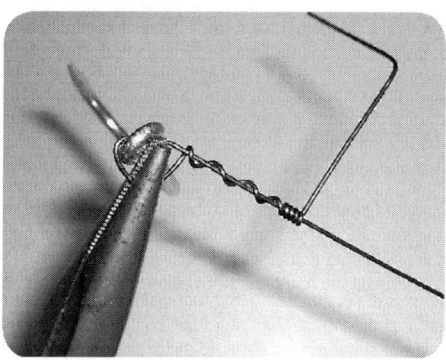

5. With your right hand, bring the tag end down, toward you, and begin to tightly wrap the tag end of the wire around the main wire. Make four complete wraps.

6. Cut the remainder of the tag end off. Or for a clean cut make a right-angle in the tag and crank clock wise once and counter clock wise once or until it breaks.

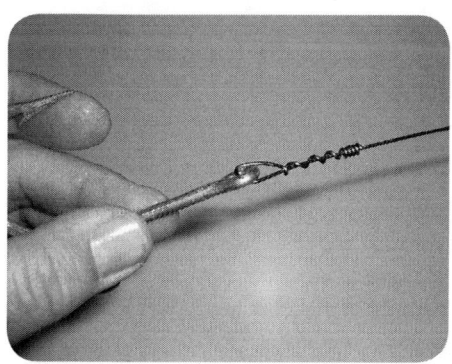

7. Measure out how many feet you want the leader to be and cut the wire.

8. Repeat the process with the other end of the wire (without a hook).

9. Note: Try not to make the loose wraps to close together. The farther apart they are, the stronger your leader will be.

Caring for your Leaders

After each use, wash your leaders and dry them off before storing them. Also spray them down with WD40. This will prevent them from rusting.

Frayed Wire or Rusted Leaders

If your leader happens to rust, throw it away. If the wire frays, you can either throw it away or try saving part of it by cutting it down and making it smaller.

Hooks

Hooks will rust after just one use or day of fishing. If you don't clean them and oil the hooks right away they will rust. I use the foraged hooks to protect the fish; this style hook will rust out in a few days saving the shark undo harm. Stainless steal hooks will take much longer to rust out.

Chum, Chum Mashers, and Chum Systems

Baiting and chumming are probably the two most important factors in attracting sharks. Two-thirds of a shark's brain is devoted to its sense of smell. For every one million particles of water, one particle of blood is enough to catch the attention of a shark. Because of this, chumming is one of the best ways to bring a shark to your boat.

The money you spend on your boat, all of your gear, fuel, oil, hooks, leaders, ice, food, and other equipment is going to be substantially more than what you spend on your bait and chum for each trip. If you feel you've already spent enough money and decide to skimp on your bait and chum, you're making a terrible mistake. There's no point in spending thousands of dollars on equipment which gets no use because you can't get a shark to come to the boat. Even if you wind up with leftover bait or chum, don't skimp in this area.

There are five methods of chumming we're also going to explore: the chum bucket, chum bag, crate system, barrel system, and chunking. To determine which is right for you, see what fits into your budget and works best with your boat.

Bait

Your choice of bait should be determined by what type of shark you are trying to catch and what bait they are feeding on in that area and time. Having a variety of choices of bait on hand can make the difference of whether or not you catch something.

Types of bait:
Tuna (Albacore, Blue fin, Yellow fin, Bonito, Skipjack)
Mackerel
Squid
Barracuda

Makos eat a lot of bonitoes. Note that bonitoes are in the tuna family. All of these tuna are good Mako bait. The head of a twenty pound tuna is good for baiting larger Makos. All tuna works well for fillet rigs/slab bait, chunking, or chumming. Bonitoes and skipjacks make good whole bait.

Mackerel, squid, and barracuda can be used for whole bait, chunk bait, and fillet rigs/slab bait. However, barracuda and squid will not work with a masher. Mackerel make good chunking bait because they are small and easy to handle.

To find a bait and chum reseller near you, call Kent Williams at NEW FISHALL BAIT CO. 1-310-532-7340

Bait to Avoid

Grinding grunions in a home blender, pouring them into milk cartons, and freezing them is a horrible experience. The only thing I ever caught using this bait was lemon sharks.

I tried grinding mackerel through a meat grinder, and dumping it into a five gallon bucket. It's almost impossible to pass a mackerel's head through a meat grinder, and the amount of work put into it is extreme. In the end, (after equipment expenses) this is more costly than buying ground mackerel.

Do not use shark as chum. The meat is so tough that it is a chore to cut it, even with a fillet knife. It's also not good practice to kill a shark to use as bait. This sort of action is highly frowned upon. Sharks are at the top of the food chain, and their job is to keep a balance in the ocean's ecosystem. It also may count as part of your catch per day limit. You can, however, use shark liver. It's very rich in oil and fairly large in size. It is generally very messy, though.

Fish carcasses do not work very well, as they are largely comprised of heads and bones. There isn't much meat or blood to actually contribute to chum.

Do not use mammal parts or blood. They are difficult to acquire, and only very large sharks (like great whites and very large Makos) generally hunt mammals. Using mammal parts will automatically disqualify you from any IGFA record.

One day when shark fishing with my buddy John and Raffa, one of his employees, we pulled up to a live bait salesman to purchase some chum buckets. Along with the buckets, the salesman offered us a 55-gallon barrel of dead sardines. We ended up taking them along with us and found the odor of the sardines to be unbearable. Raffa was out for his first sharking experience and he was very excited to be joining us. As we approached the shark grounds, the smell started to get to us, and we knew couldn't deal with it much longer. We coerced Raffa to begin chumming the sardines, so we could use them for the chum slick. John and I decided to get as far away from the sardines as possible and went to the bow of the boat. Meanwhile, Raffa was being such a trooper; he dealt with the sardines for hours on end, not once complaining about the odor. John and I joked around about it, because we knew that Raffa was thinking he probably wouldn't be invited on another sharking trip if he complained, which of course was not true. We didn't see a single shark the entire day, not even a blue, and I realized that the bait we used was tainted. I think that bait salesman suckered us into taking his dead sardines to sea to dump them for him. The moral of this story is, never use tainted bait!

Great White meal of leftover sea lion parts

WHERE TO PURCHASE BAIT AND CHUM

 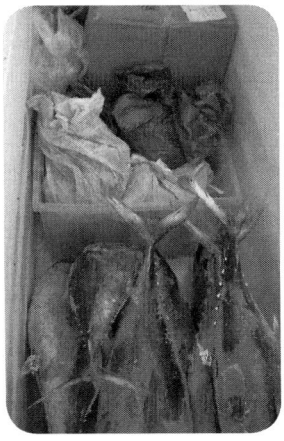 

If you wish to store your own bait you will need plenty of freezer space

Most of your local fuel docks or bait resellers at the docks sell dead, frozen squid, mackerel, and chum buckets, an easy place to obtain your bait and chum. There are manufacturers that specialize in producing blocks and four gallon (33-pound) buckets of special blend chum. These cost between $10 and $40 per piece.

You can contact your local fishery, cannery, or wholesale fish distributor and purchase whole mackerel, squids, and tuna. This can make a big difference in your catches, as you actually know what is in your chum. This bait is slightly cheaper, but there are still expenses involved in storing your excess fish/chum and using a barrel system to dispense it.

How to Store Bait

Individually bag each of your fish, keep them separated, or group them by the amount you want to take out per trip. It's a real burden dealing with fish frozen together and having to break them apart.

TIP: Don't use the freezer you store your food in as the bait will smell everything up.

How to Prepare Bait and Chum Before a Trip

Factor in the outside air temperature, water temperature, and travel time prior to putting the bait or chum into the water. You don't want the bait or chum to be too frozen, nor too thawed out (unless it's going into the chum barrel where you will mash it). Odor is also a factor. In some cases, you may need to remove the bait and chum from the freezer the night before your trip, so you can begin the thawing process. If it's very warm outside and/or you will be in direct sunlight, don't leave your bait out for too long. If it turns to mush, it will be very hard to use as hook or slab bait. On the flipside, if it's too cold and you get out to the shark grounds with frozen bait, it's nearly impossible to work with. Like an ice cube, frozen mackerel will float on the surface of the water.

Storing Bait on the Boat

Don't leave bait out in direct sunlight, unless it's going into the barrel. Try to keep it cold, fresh, and well thawed, leaving it on ice if need be. If a block or bucket is being used, take extra caution to leave it in a cool, shady place, or you risk having it thaw prematurely and dispense too quickly. If you use my barrel system however, it doesn't matter if the fish is thawed or not, since it's going to be mashed anyway.

Dispensing Units

1. Chum Bucket

This is the easiest and cleanest method of chumming, with almost no effort involved. Purchase a chum bucket, cut some flaps and holes for rope into the lid, and tie it to the boat. Rather than cutting holes, make *adjustable,* V-shaped flaps so you can control the rate of chum flow. When you cut a hole into the bucket, you are stuck with what you have.

Don't tie your rope to the wire handle of the bucket. If the bucket hits the bottom of the boat or is pulled hard enough, the handle will come off and the bucket will drift away or sink. Cut holes for your rope, one on the lid and one the side of the bucket. This will secure the lid. Run the rope through the side of the bucket and through the lid, with the bucket hole a couple inches from the corner of the short side of the bucket.

2. Floating Crate

A floating crate is exactly what its name implies, a crate that floats in the water. You can either use block chum or set a chum bucket upside down (with lid removed) to disperse your chum. For trolling, it can be towed alongside or behind the boat. A floating crate disperses chum faster than a bucket, but not quite as fast as a chum barrel.

To make a floating crate, add tube-shaped, rubber or foam padding to all four top-sides of a milk crate, securing the padding with tie wraps. Tie a rope a couple inches from the corner of the top, short side of the crate. This allows the crate to drift nicely and troll at the proper angle.

3. Chum Barrel

The chum barrel system offers the greatest flexibility and control. It allows you to manually adjust the water/chum ratio and disperse rate. The chum barrel system is basically a custom barrel with inflow and outflow control. For details and more information on making one, see the *Barrel System* chapter.

4. Chum Bag
The chum bag that I use is a regular diving bag that you could purchase at any dive shop. I tie it off to the boat and load it up with cut bait or cut shark liver. Leave the bag in the water to give you a continuous scent trail while you are drifting.

5. Chunking
Use chunking with all three of the methods listed above, any time you shark fish. Chunking is cutting up bait into "chunks" and periodically tossing them overboard into the depths of the water. The purpose of chunking is to get the scent deep in the water. While oil slicks and particles from slicking stay at the surface, chunking calls to sharks from the depths of the ocean to the surface. If you want to increase your chances of bringing a shark to the surface by more than fifty percent, start chunking from the beginning to end. I highly recommend this practice every time you go out sharking. Mackerel are the easiest fish for chunking, since they are so easy to cut.

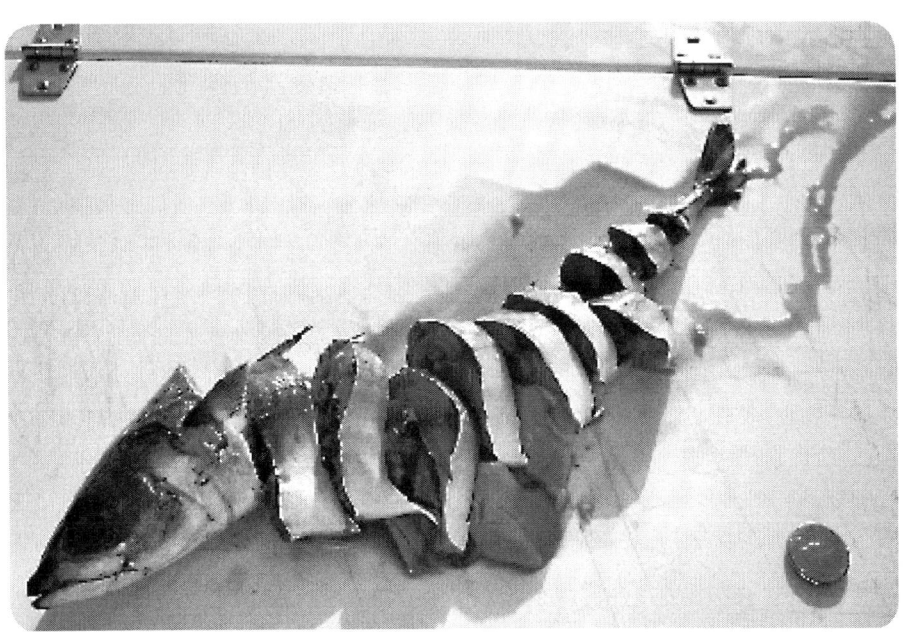

When you cut your bait, make sure your chunks are large enough to sink to the bottom, but not large enough to serve as a meal.

> NOTE: All drift bait rigging should be done with 400–1000 pound cables and 10/0 to 14/0 hooks.

The Brew (Attractants) - Mixtures

While there are many attractants available for adding to your chum: fish pellets, vegetable oil, fish oil, mammal oil, animal parts, rice, cat food, dog food. If you use the barrel system, most of these are unnecessary. I prefer to stick to bait on which Makos actually feed.

High oil content is the key to getting your chum system to work. If you're using the barrel system, make sure to use fish with high oil contents (tuna and mackerel). If you use the bucket system, make sure the fish in it have high oil content.

Drift Chumming

One thing you never want to do while out in the water is break your slick. While you drift, it's always a good idea to continue to lay slick and chunk. If you are using the barrel system, always make sure your pump is working. It could be helpful to have a backup system for chumming or chunking just in case, such as a bucket tied alongside the boat to dispense small amounts of chum.

Chum Mashers

You can either purchase a preassembled masher or build your own. A good masher can make your day easy; a low-quality masher will give you a sore arm.

"Homemade" Mashers

A. Tile Scraper

You can use a tile scraper as a chum masher. A standard tile scraper has a four-foot handle and a six-inch blade. While this will work, it will give you a hard time. Due to its light weight, a lot of force is needed to mash chum.

B. Wooden Baseball Bat with Five-pound, Iron Dumbbell Weight Attachment

You can use a wooden baseball bat with a five-pound, iron dumbbell bolted on the end. This was my first chum mashing method. The bat provides more leverage than a tile scraper, but it is very difficult to mash chum with it due to the very blunt edge.

C. My Custom-Made System
I have found this masher to be the most efficient and comfortable, as well as the easiest to use. It gives a lot of leverage and is sharp enough to mash chum easily. Due to its unique shape and weight, this masher makes it very easy to mix the chum. All you have to do is lift the masher a few times, and it thoroughly mixes the contents of the barrel with little effort.

Parts Needed for Building Masher:
All parts are stainless steel

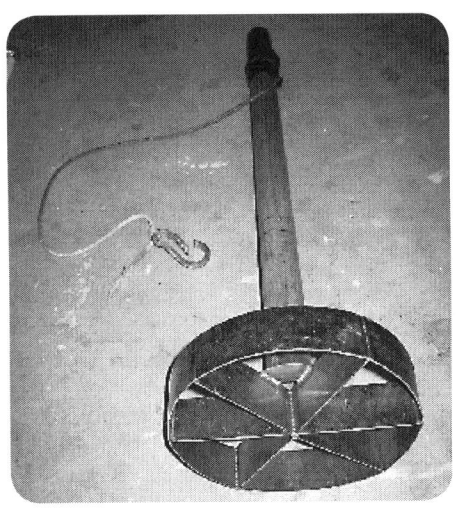

A. 1 ¾" x 34" tube
B. 1 ¾" diameter x 1/16" round sheet of metal
C. 3 ½" x 1/16" round ring
D. 32" x 1/16" x 2" flat sheet of metal (this will be made into the outer ring later)
E. 6 fins, each 4 ⅞" x 1/16" x 2"
F. 36" rope & d-clip
G. Electrical tape

Construction of Masher:
1. Weld B to one end of A.
2. Weld C to the center of the other end of A.
3. Form D into a circular ring, and weld together.
4. Weld E every 6" on D.
5. Once all 6 fins are welded to the ring, weld them at the center.

6. Tie a rope 5 ½" from the top of the tube, and wrap the top 8" with electrical tape (over the rope).
7. Attach the clip to the other end of the rope. (This is a safety line, so you don't accidentally lose it overboard. The clip can be attached anywhere you want, as long as it's sturdy and secure.)

Alternative Model:

All parts are stainless steel
A. 1 ¼" x 36" tube
B. 1 ¼" diameter x ⅛ " round sheet of metal
C. 4 fins, each 3 ¼" x 3 ¼" x ⅛"

Construction of Alternative Model:

1. Weld b to one end of A.
2. Sharpen one end of each of the 4 fins.
3. Weld all 4 fins C evenly onto the other end of A, with the sharpened ends facing down.
4. Tie a rope 5 ½" from the top of the tube and wrap the top 8" with electrical tape (over the rope).

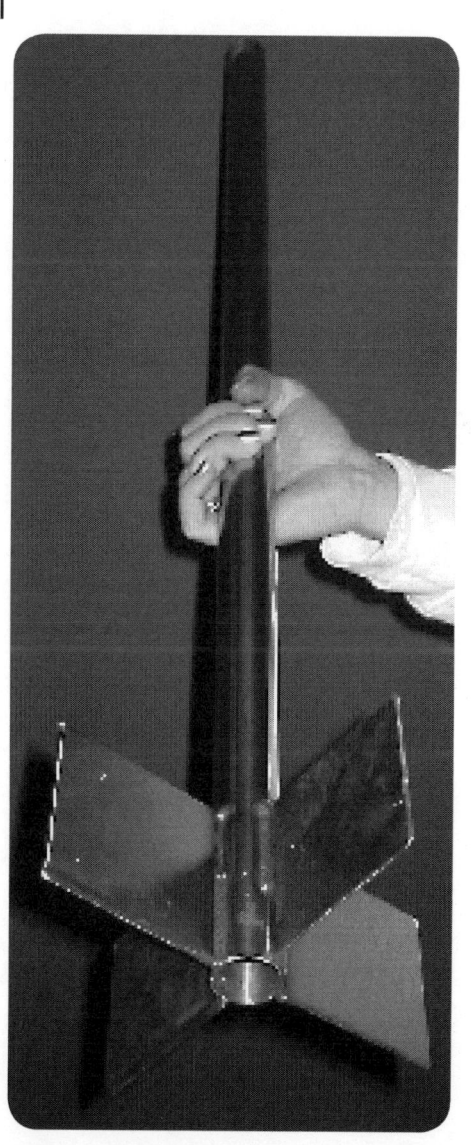

To order either one of these chum mashers call C & D Welding, ask for Darren at 1-666-259-4780

Barrel System

Before we look at the chum ratios, it is very important to understand the chum system itself because Mako sharks are warm-blooded, apex predators. They are always looking for the freshest (dead or alive) bait.

Over the years, I've experimented with many types of systems. One of the first ones I tried was the chum bucket system. The bucket system works very well, but sometimes you don't know what kind of fish are in the bucket. This can lead to many problems, like long days with nothing other than blue sharks coming to the boat, or nothing coming period. If you're going to use the chum bucket system, make sure you know (from your provider) what kind of fish are inside. That is the key to a viable chum bucket.

There are many advantages to using my chum system. I've spent many years perfecting it, and through personal experience I can tell you this is a simple chum solution. It is definitely a lot of work, but the payoff of using this system is ten times better than traditional methods. It's awarded me seven placements in seven consecutive tournaments.

My System

Time is of the essence when you are shark fishing. It may take you hours to get to your fishing grounds, to set up and prepare, plus there's the return travel time, clean up of gear, and more. You want to be as efficient as possible with your time. A frozen bucket of chum takes a big bite out of your time.

My barrel system is a very effective method for maximizing the best output of chum into the water. It is also very easy to use. I like to get a chum barrel flowing and lay down a half-mile slick before I stop at my selected fishing site. This quickly rings the dinner bell for sharks in the area.

The chum barrel is capable of laying down 10 to 15 gallons of mixed chum and water in a mile pre-slick, depending on how thick you want the slick. With a 20 to 40 dollar frozen bucket, you probably won't want to dump it all in the first half mile. I used to drag a bucket a half mile, getting minimal slick out of it (half a gallon or less would be dissipated out of the bucket). With the barrel system, you can release larger quantities of chum. Dispense five to ten gallons in your first half-mile to mile before you stop on your drift.

This is the most critical part in starting a successful day of shark fishing! If you just drop the entire bucket into your fishing spot, it could take many hours before a shark swims into the slick, if it comes at all. With my method you may even spot them before you get your fishing lines into the water.

Water-Chum Ratios

A 30-gallon barrel with this design allows 25 gallons of water to be in the system already. The recommended amount of chum for starting the barrel is 20 to 30 pounds. The recommended amount of chum for any day of shark fishing should not exceed 100 to 300 pounds.

Starting the Barrel
1. 20 pounds of whole tuna and 6-10 mackerel or 25 to 30 pounds of whole mackerel.
- All bait should be at least half thawed for best results.
2. Check the solidity of the mixture, and try to maintain this solidity for the rest of the day.
- If you decide to cut the heads off your bait (e.g. baiting hooks), do not throw them into sea, as it will feed the sharks.

Supplies for Making a 30-gallon Barrel
1. Barrel - 30 gallon, standard, plastic barrel, roughly 19" length by 30" height
2. Pump - Ordinary bait system or raw water wash down pump Recommended: 3.8 or 4.3 gallons per minute (gpm)
3. Hose shutoff - Plastic or zinc hose shutoff with fingertip flow control

4. Hose (inflow) – Kink-proof garden hose, with an extra female connector You will need one additional female connector for installation. Length is determined by how far your pump is from your barrel.
5. Hose (outflow) - 1 ¾" x 6 ft. rigged
6. Inflow Connector - Nylon male garden hose ¾ to ¾" nut
7. Outflow Connector - 1 ¾ x 3 ¾" plastic mushroom head (barbed)
8. Drain plug (optional)
9. 1 tube of silicon

Patent Pending

NOTE: If you feel 30 gallons is overkill for you, you can make your barrel size anywhere from 5 gallons to 30, as your needs may differ. My first barrel was 5 gallons and I worked my way up to the 30 gallon I use today.

Construction and Installation of the Barrel System

There are many steps involved in building and installing your barrel system. Each step is critical for success.

Preparing the Barrel

Before you begin installation of the parts, position your barrel on your boat to allow you to decide where you want to make the drills for inflow, outflow, and the drain plug.

1. You will need to cut a lid on the barrel using a Sawzall. Be sure not to cut the top of the barrel itself. The best place to make the cut is the inside top of the barrel.
2. Drill a ¾" hole for water inflow fitting, 3½" from the top of the barrel (left side). Install your nylon male garden hose to the outside of the barrel, and the fastening nut on the inside.
3. Drill a 1 ¾" hole for the outflow fitting, 7" from the top of the barrel (right side).

   a. Install silicon against the backing of the mushroom head, which will be installed from the inside of the barrel. Be sure to use A LOT of silicon.

   b. Install mushroom head into the hole (from the inside of the barrel), passing the barbs and the threaded area to the outside of the barrel.

   c. Install silicon over the threaded area, on the outside of the barrel, only where the threaded area is physically touching the outside of the bucket. Be sure to use a lot of silicon here as well.

   d. Attach the 1 ¾" x 3 ft hose over the plastic mushroom head. It should slip easily right over the barb.
4. Drain plug (optional)
5. Fastening the barrel to the boat - the most critical part, as the location you install it determines many things, such as the length of the water intake hose you will need, the drainage hose.

Materials needed: Standard dock ropes work fine, but I recommend using tie downs, or both. Tie downs are faster and more efficient. It's also very easy to install or uninstall.

Places you can install the barrel- Swim step or deck.

Parts Needed for Mounting
1. 2 U-Bolts (swim set mounting only)
2. Tie downs (2+) and/or 2 dock lines. Any size should be sufficient.

> TIP: If you can, mount the barrel on the swim step.

Swim Step Mounting
Before you consider swim step mounting, you need to make sure your swim step can accommodate the weight of the full barrel and force being applied to it. Factor in chum, water, pounding of sea, and chum mixing. Don't forget about boat speed or swells, either.

25 gallons water + 30 pounds chum
8.3 pounds per gallon of water
207.5 pounds water + 30 pounds chum = 237.5 pound bucket

1. Install 2 U-Bolts through the transom, one on each side of where the barrel is going to rest.
2. Install the tie downs to reinforce the barrel, by tying each end to a U-Bolt. I recommend at least 2, so you can have one for reinforcement.
3. Install the hose shutoff either on the pump, your boats raw water wash down connection, or the barrel itself.
4. Check what length inflow hose you will need.
5. Cut excess length off of male side of hose, and attach the female connector to the hose.
6. Make sure the hose is attached to the pump and barrel, along with secure fasteners.
7. Install the 1 ¾" rigged outflow hose, and cut to desired length.
8. Test the system to see that it is not leaking.

Deck Mounting

If you choose to install on the deck, follow these instructions.

1. The bottom of the barrel to the bottom of the outflow hose measures 22 inches. If your gunnel is higher than 22 inches from the deck, elevate the barrel or open the transom door so that the outflow hose reaches over the gunnel. You can use plastic carts, large plastic bowls, block of wood, or anything else that is convenient for you.
2. Once you've reached the desired height, fasten the barrel with tie downs from the stern cleat, around the barrel, and back to the cleat. If access to a cleat is not available, any other fastening method would work, as all boats vary.
3. Follow steps 3-8 from the swim step mounting instructions.

PRE-SLICKING AND POWER CHUMMING

As a general rule for shark fishing, it is unfair and impractical to expect any one person to do everything. As you do your pre-slicking and power chumming, make sure each crew member's duties are clear. It is practical and efficient to have one crew member operate the barrel, one chunking, and someone feeding bait to the bait system operators.

Pre-Slicking

1. Before Leaving Dock
Add weight to your barrel at the dock to help keep it secure. If you're putting any frozen chum in the barrel, this will allow time for it to thaw before you reach your fishing spot. You want enough weight to keep the barrel from moving around, but not so much that the barrel can be thrown overboard or can damage your boat while underway.

Lighter greasy discoloration is the chum slick

2. Leaving Harbor, Heading Toward Destination

In most cases, you are heading 20 or more miles offshore. Always keep an eye out for better fishing areas. It's possible that before you reach your fishing spot you will find signs of life, or sharks finning on a good current break. Because of this, you may decide that you want to change your fishing spot.

3. At Desired Fishing Location

Once you reach your desired fishing location, check for the proper signs. If you don't like your first spot, move on to your second choice.

4. After Finding a Fishing Location

If everything is good, stop the boat. Now the work begins!

a. Start filling the barrel (with chum and water). Shut off water when the water level reaches six inches below the outflow hose.

b. Check wind direction and ocean current direction.

c. Let boat drift and note the direction of the drift.

d. After determining the direction of the drift, head in the opposite direction of the drift, for half a mile to one mile.

5. Mile Past Fishing Spot

Once you reach about a mile away, turn the water on, and fill the barrel completely, so that the chum starts to come out. This is the beginning point of your slick.

6. Pre-Slicking:

Now that you have chum coming out of your barrel, head back to your fishing spot at 4-8 knots, while making sure to lay down a good slick. You may need to add extra water to your barrel to expel the proper proportions of chum. The faster you are traveling, the higher the water/chum output you will need. Continue slicking until you reach your fishing spot. While doing this, you should be chunking as well.

7. Back at Fishing Spot

Shut off motors and start drifting. This concludes the pre-slicking process.

**Example of a pre-slicking route.
The High Spot is marked at 499 on the map.**

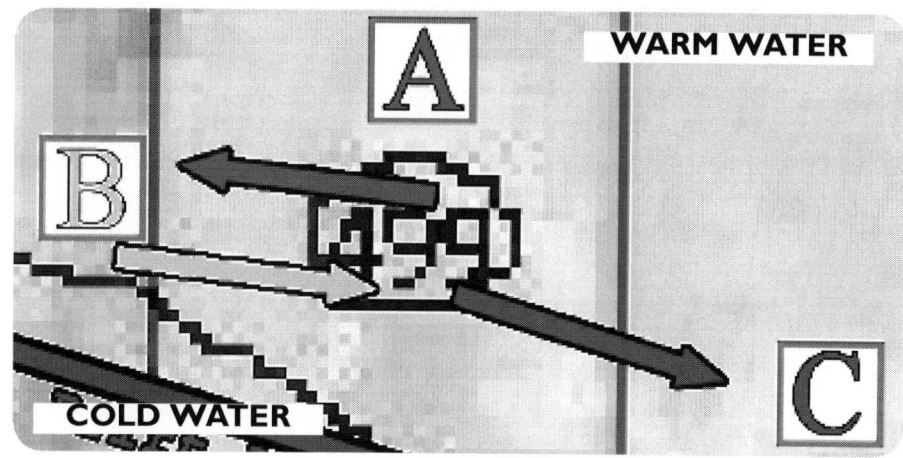

Notice the cool water with a current break on both sides of it and warm water on the 499 high spot. Note the drift line and the direction it's going to take your boat. Go directly to the high spot. If the conditions look good and you want to fish it, go to B (cooler area), begin your pre-slicking; stop pre-slicking back at the high spot A and start your drift toward C.

Maintaining the Barrel
1. Mix thoroughly; pound to a nice blend.
2. Mix barrel every 10 minutes.
3. Add twenty or more mackerel or tuna every 30 minutes.

The bottom several inches of the barrel will contain a very solid layer of fish. You need to add mackerel or tuna so that you can have additional blood and oil particles in the mixture, as blood and oil are able to escape the barrel quicker than solid chunks and particles. Sometimes, additional water is added via a high-pressure wash down hose to mix the chum and/or increase the chum output.

It is very important that you mix the barrel every 10 minutes, because the heavier materials sink to the bottom.

Power Chumming

When there is no drift, you will want to do some power chumming in addition to your pre-slicking. When power chumming, you don't want to fish one area for too long when there is no drift. Every 30 minutes or so, it's a good idea to move a half mile to a mile and lay down some more chum and slick. You should continue to do so to cover more area. Move in the same direction as the drift. If you have a chum bucket out in the water, when you start your motor make sure the bucket doesn't get in the way of the propellers.

Tying Lines & Hooks

Introduction

It is critical that you learn to properly rig your bait. The proper knot being tied can make the difference between catching and not catching. Make sure you retie your knots every time you use that outfit. These two knots are the basic shark knots that I use.

Knots

A. Double Knot - used for tying mono line 30 lb to 130 lb to swivels. A great amount of pressure is necessary to make this knot. You will need to attach the swivel to something that will not move.

1. Double the line back about 24".

2. Hold the main line and the tag end in your right hand. The double backed looped end should be in your left hand.

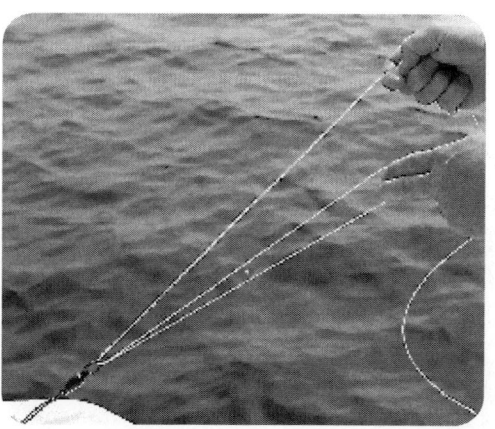

3. Feed the double backed looped end through the ring on the swivel. Make sure you do not twist the line. You should be holding the doubled backed looped end in your left hand and the main line with the tag end in your right hand.

4. Loop the double backed looped end over your fingers on your right hand.

5. Pass the double backed tag end under the main line.

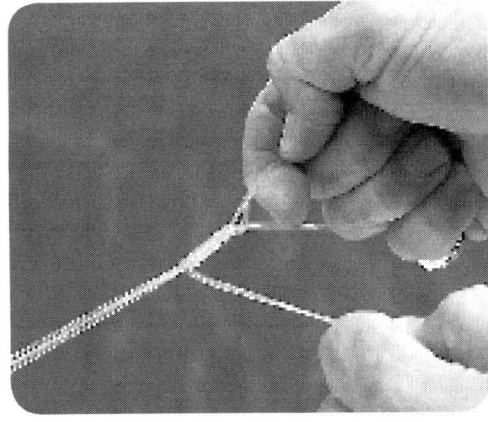

6. Take the doubled backed loop end and make 9 wraps over the main line.

7. Keep all wraps neat without crossing or twisting.

8. You can hold your coils with your right thumb/hand so that it does not unravel on this next step. Or you can perform this next step and bring the coils tight again.

9. Thread the double backed looped end through the first loop above the eye of the swivel. Pull coils tight to your right hand.

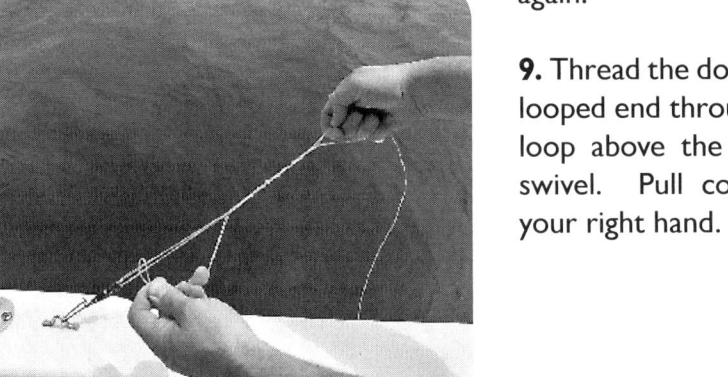

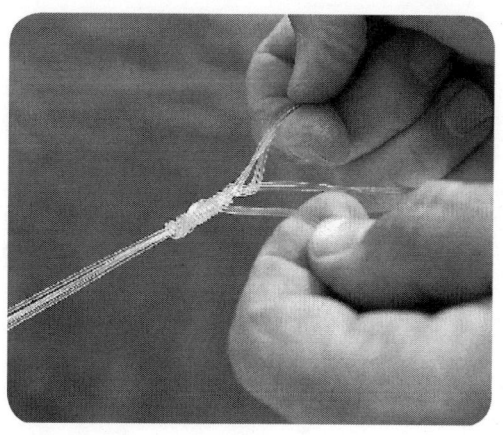

10. Pull the tag end up against the coils making them tight. Then let the tag end wind back over the coils once.

11. Holding the coils in place, pass the tag end through the loop created by the line held in your fingers. Now remove your fingers from the loop and pull the knot tight.

12. Wet the loops and remove your fingers from the loop and pull the knot tight.

13. Hold the tag end and main line while pulling up the coils. The coils should be in a spiral, and not overlapping each other. Slide the knot down to the eye of your swivel by pulling both the main line and the looped tag end until the knot is tight.

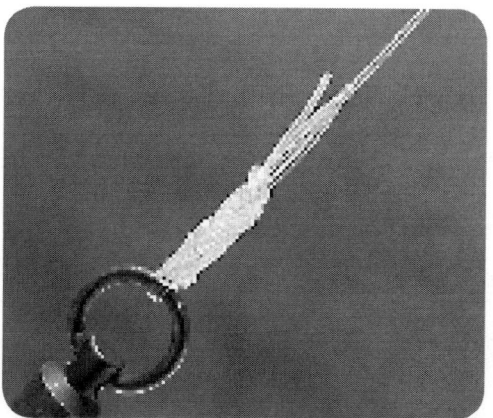

14. Make sure your double line is not overlapping on the ring of the swivel and that all of your wraps are nice and even throughout.

15. Cut tag ends off.

16. This is a finished double shark knot.

B. Cats Paw/Swivel to Double Knot - used for tying Dacron line to swivels

1. Thread the loop end of your double through the eye of the snap swivel and pass the swivel through the loop and twist the line once.

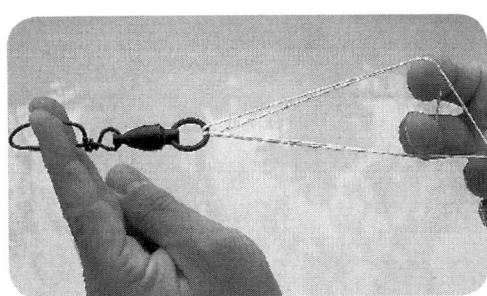

2. Fold the loop end of the double back against the standing part of the loop.

3. Rotate the swivel through the central loop formed. Do this from four to six times depending on the thickness and pliability of the line.

4. Close up the knot. Take your time easing the knot down to the swivel.

Rigging Bait

Dead Bait

Dead bait is very practical for shark fishing because it is easy to obtain. You can catch and dispatch your own bait fish or buy them ready to store for later use. I've always been able to catch sharks with dead bait, and prefer them to live bait ten to one because it is easier to acquire fresh dead bait.

Since Mako sharks are predators and not scavengers, they prefer fresh meals. This makes using the freshest bait possible very important. Just because Makos prefer live bait, it doesn't mean that dead bait won't work. It's simply a matter of tricking the shark into thinking the bait is alive or has been recently attacked.

If you see a shark investigating your bait and not taking it, pick up your rod and reel and pop the line several times to make your bait jump. This will give the illusion that the bait is alive. When Mako sharks think your bait is alive, they will go for it. If the shark will not eat, try feeding it. Throw the shark slab bait or chunks, try and get it to feed. Once the shark starts feeding it then will most likely take your hook bait.

A. Tuna Heads

The tuna head system is designed strictly for larger fish. You want your hook to be as tight and secure as possible, so when the boat is moving through the swell and tugging on the head, the pressure is not applied to the hook, but to the securely tied cable. This is done to prevent displacement of the hook and to prevent the hooks position from changing.

1. For tuna heads, use a 10 to 20 pound albacore, bluefin, or yellowfin head. When I cut tuna heads, I cut from the top of the head (behind the gill plate) down toward the front of the pectoral fin to the ventral fin. Alternatively, you can exaggerate the cut from the pectoral fin all the way to the anal fin. I do this so that smaller fish that feed on the bait don't mutilate the head. This is a particularly good idea on a day where lots of small sharks are feeding.

2. Before you set the hook through the head, take the hook and wire leader and set them up against the top of head to determine where to insert the hook. The loop of wire leader should line up with the eyes of the tuna head.

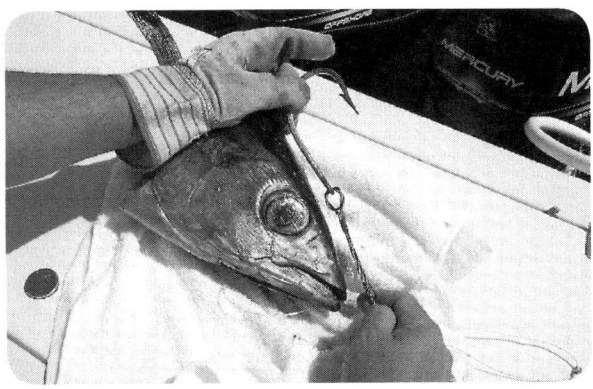

3. Insert the hook into the tuna head. The hook is most commonly placed somewhere behind the eye. When you bring the hook out the other end, make sure the loop from the wire leader is just above the eye of the head.

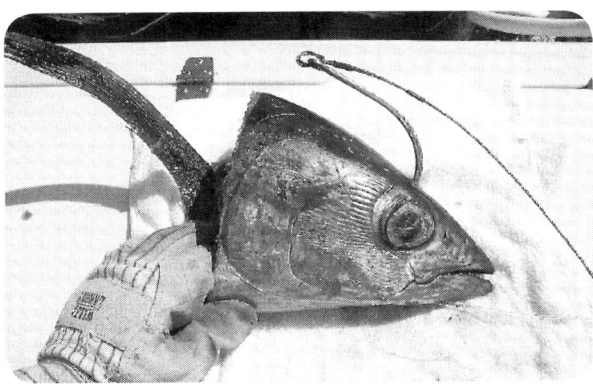

4. Get a 12 inch Dacron line ready to tie the leader to the tuna head.

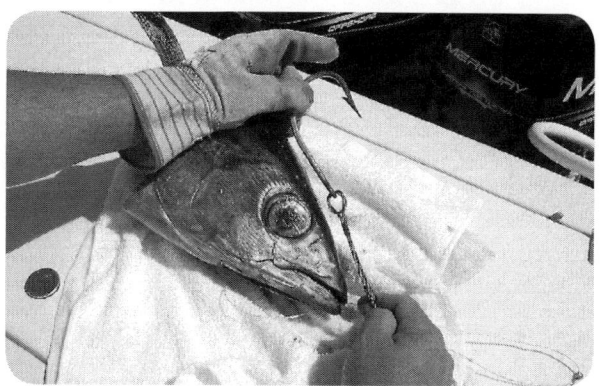

5. Take the 12 inches of Dacron line and put it through the eye of a needle, with six inches coming out of each end. Place the needle through one eye of the head and out the other eye, pulling one end of the string out the other end. You should have six inches of line coming out of each side of the fish.

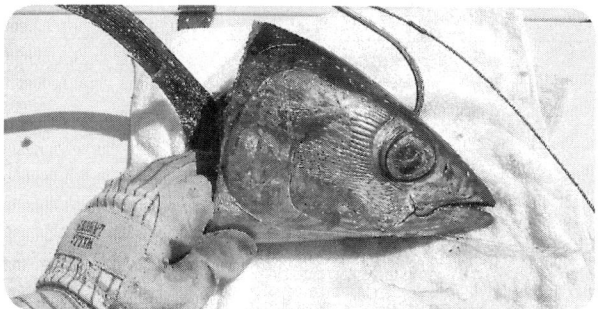

6. Remove the needle and pass the line through the ring on the leader, tying the leader securely to the head.

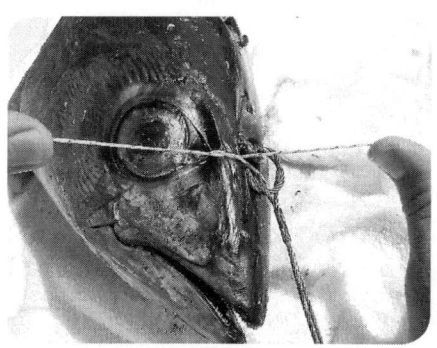
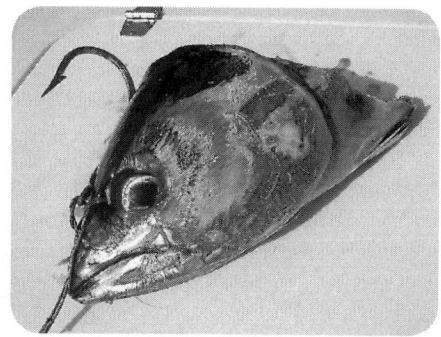

B. Whole Tuna

For large skipjacks 3 to 5 lbs (or any other tuna around this size), use the same procedure as the tuna head. You can choose to use only the head or the entire fish and still use the same method. If you choose to use the entire fish, have the hook pass out through the back of the fish with the barb coming out at the dorsal fin. Like the tuna heads, skipjacks are used solely for big fish. It is a good idea to cut a few slits into the fish for added scent.

Follow these instructions:

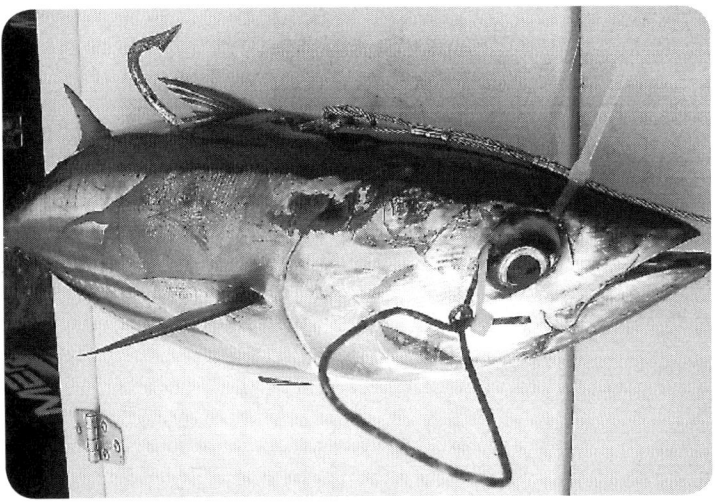

1. Pass the hook through the top of the back of the tuna near the dorsal fin.

2. Pull the leader tight and pass a tie wrap through the eyes of the tuna. Then bring the tie wrap up and over the leader, cinch it down hard. Then cut the reaming tag end off the tie wrap.

3. Make an incision through the rough and the bottom of the mouth. Run a tie wrap through the upper and lower part of the mouth and over the wire leader. Cinch the tie wrap down over the leader closing tight the mouth of the tuna.

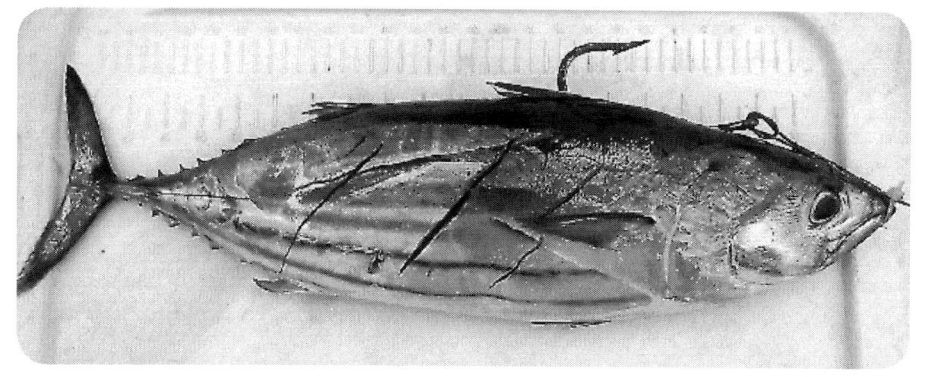

4. Cut slits in the bait when done rigging it for more scent and blood trails.

In some cases I run another piece of cable 10 to 12 inches long. Crimp it from the main hook at the loop area of the cable to another hook. And then I place this hook further back and on the bottom of the tuna in the annul fin area. This two hook setup just might pay off; it's more work but could have huge rewards.

C. Giant Squid

Giant squid can be used to catch anything that weighs from 70 to 700 pounds. It most definitely is a nasty smelling bait to use. But, bait scent is good. Even more importantly you can make the squid look alive by popping the line with your rod. The tentacles will move giving the appearance to the shark that the squid is alive.

1. Run the hook and cable through one inch from the tip of the squid and out at hook length.

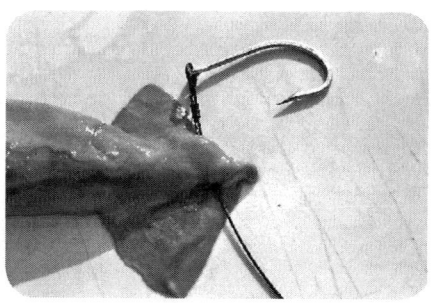

2. Pull the hook and cable through the tip to the head. Do not run the cable inside the body of the squid. The reason I do not run the cable inside of the squid is sometimes the sharks teeth will pull the squid down over the hook. This will prevent you from setting the hook. If the cable is on the outside, the hook will generally never get covered up by the squid, hence allowing for a hook set.

3. Pass the hook through the bulb of the squid head; it should be far back enough so that the hook can pass through the back end of the head, near tentacles. This disguises the hook as a tentacle.

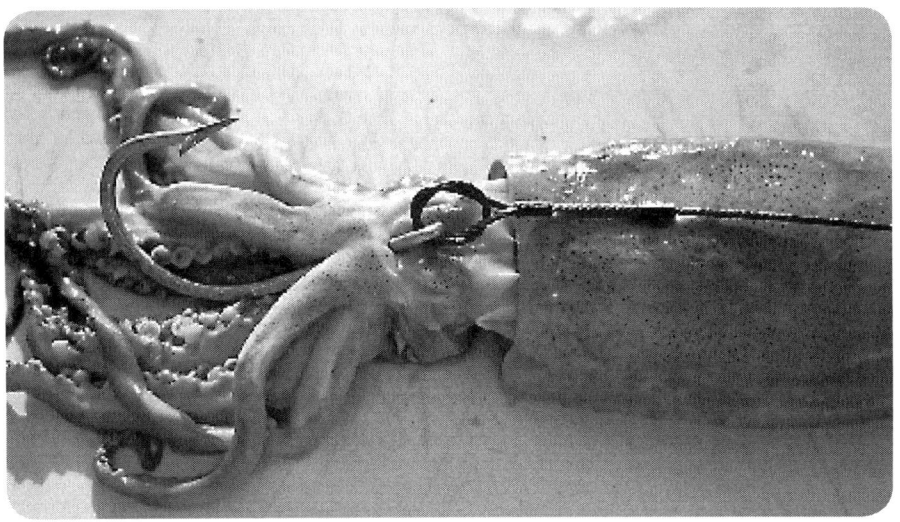

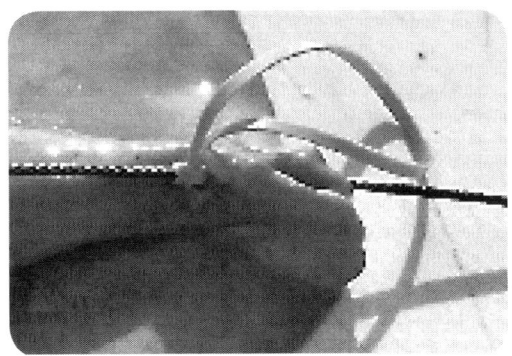

4. To prevent the squid from drooping, loop a rubber band under the cable in between the first insert and pass the rubber band through itself, pulling it very tight.

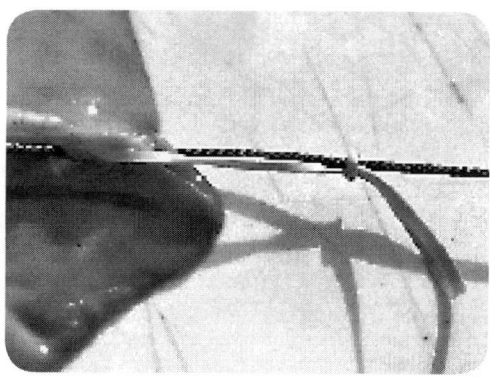

5. Tie the open end of the rubber band to the cable two inches up past the top of the squid. It is crucial that you make the knot very tight, as the rubber band should not be able to slide up and down.
6. This a completed shark squid bait.

D. Mackerel

Mackerel can be used to catch the smallest 40 pound shark to a monster of any size. There are numerous ways to rig a mackerel. Refer to rigging dead mackerel (small or large, as necessary), with these tips in mind.

1. Live mackerel should be pinned through the nose. This makes it easy to pull through the water while drifting.
2. If there is no drift, you can pin it in the back or anal area.
3. If you have a Mako at the back of the boat, pin it through the hard part of the nose. Cut the entire tail off the mackerel so that it bleeds profusely. Toss the bait directly in front of the Mako.

Small Mackerel

A 10/0 or 12/0 hook is too big to bury into small mackerel bait. Here are three simple methods you can use with a 7/0.

1 Nose hook: Run the hook through the bottom of the jaw up through the bony nose area. The nose hook is best if you are looking for a quick job.

2 Top: Run the hook through the bottom of the jaw and bring it out through the bony nose. Run it again, from the top of the mackerel to the dorsal fin, placing rubber bands around the hook, cable, and body of the mackerel. Run one rubber band every few inches.

3. Bottom: Run the hook through the top of the bony area of the nose and out the bottom of the jaw. You can use rubber bands to secure the hook near the anal fin. Place a rubber band every few inches around the hook and cable.

4. Belly: Run the hook through the mouth, bend the mackerel around the hook, and work the hook and pass it out through the anal fin area. Tie the mouth shut with dental floss or a tie wrap.

Large Mackerel
1. Top: Run the hook through the dorsal fin area. Insert the hook again through the top of the mackerel and out the dorsal fin. Use one rubber band to tie the nose.

2. Bottom: Run the hook through the top of the bony area of the nose and out the bottom of the jaw. Run the hook again through the anal fin and bring it out at hook's length. Use one rubber band to tie the nose.

Fillet Rigs/Slab Bait

Making the fillet (Large bait and cables)

1. To bait large Makos, use whole bellies of tuna and or a side-cut off of tuna.

   Belly: Use a complete belly from a 10 to 20 pound tuna.

When you remove the belly, it should resemble a diamond shape. This seems to give the fillet a more natural look as it's dragged through the water.

2. Pass the hook in and out through one end and pierce it through the opposing end. After passing it through once, turn the hook around and bring it out the other end. The tip of the hook should be facing toward where you made your first insertion. The shank should be resting flat on the fillet.
3. Use a rubber band or tie wrap to secure the fillet to the cable.
4. Side slab: When cutting a slab, one end should always be narrower than the other. This helps it pull through the water.
5. Insert the hook into the tip of the narrow end of the slab.
6. Turn the hook around and pass it through again, at hook's length. The tip of the hook should be facing the narrow end of the slab.

Making the fillet (small bait and solid wire leaders)
1. Cut diagonally from behind the head and across the backbone through the end of the fish. Including the tail is optional.
2. Pass the hook through the thick end of the fillet.
3. Twist the hook and pass it back through the top of the fillet.
4. The barb should be facing the front of the fillet.

Sea Monsters

If you see a sea monster in your slick, quickly bait a large slab on the thick end and toss it to him. Let the slab flutter down in front of his face. Reel it back in if he does not take it, and try it again.

Live Bait

Whenever practical, try to obtain some live bait, though it's not a necessity to be successful. There are some days when Makos only go for live bait. Sometimes when a Mako is chasing live bait, the live bait will escape the Mako. You may want to cut the tail off the bait so it doesn't get away. If you cut the tail, make sure not to cut too far up or the fish will die very quickly. If you see a Mako finning, cutting your bait's tail off and slow troll in front of the shark, or run up to the bow and cast on top of the shark, using bait with the tail cut off.

An interesting Mako trait is that these sharks first attack their prey from the rear, biting off the prey's tail, and then they circles around to go for the rest. If after biting the bait, the Mako notices something unnatural, it can be spooked.

TIP: If the bait is nose hooked, a Mako could easily grab the bait and pull it off the hook. Give the Mako more time to eat nose-hooked bait before you go for a hook set.

Trolling and Downrigger Fishing

If you don't want to deal with the hassle of chumming, trolling is an easy alternative. I used to do a lot of trolling for Makos, but not anymore. Larger Makos will usually not bite small lures, so trolling usually produces only smaller Makos. I primarily troll for threshers, as threshers of all sizes will hit trolled lures.

Some lures are rigged with a double hook. This setup is great for threshers but not so good for Makos. On many occasions I have caught Makos on the double hook but instead of getting a hook set, the rig snagged in the Mako's jaw and came unbuttoned. The Mako may come back and hit the rig again. The factory-made double hook setup is usually not spaced far enough apart; with bait on it, this rig tends to bunch up in the Mako's mouth. Over the years I have learned alternate ways to rig lures to allow an easy hook set in the Mako jaws.

Threshers, however, respond well to the usual manufacturer setup. Threshers will whack the lures with their tails for a good hook set.

When you do get a hook up on a Mako or thresher don't stop the boat. Throttle it up to about 6 to 8 knots, as if you were marlin fishing. This will help with the hook set and moves the fish away from your other lines.

Trolling and Downrigger Trolling

First find the fishiest area that might produce the right conditions for trolling. Find the thermocline on your sonar and troll just above it. Look for bait balls on your sonar as well. Once you find bait balls, troll that area making adjustments to your depths that will run the lures through the bait balls. Look for birds working an area; a shark feeding on bait can push the bait to the surface where it can become an easy feast for birds.

Recommended Lures and Bait for Trolling

1. Surface lures
Marlin lure: Add wire leader
Braid Morodor: Add wire leader
CD18 Rapala: Add wire leader

2. Deep diving lures
Baitomatic: Add live or dead mackerel
Top Gun: Add live or dead mackerel

3. Downriggers
Baitomatic: Add live or dead mackerel
Top Gun: Add live or dead mackerel
Rapala

The trolling spread can very depending on the boat's configuration capabilities. For threshers, troll one to three knots and for Makos, two to four knots.

Setting Up the Spread

Setup and Preparation

So you've found your grounds, finished pre-slicking, stopped the boat, and got your chum flowing. What's next? The first thing I do when I arrive at the sharking grounds is turn my boat's engines off and take several minutes to reflect upon what's ahead. Before the adventure beings, I just take a break. I think about the speed of the drift, and who can/will do which shipboard jobs. I take a mental inventory of everything we have and what needs to start happening to get set up. I determine which gear I need to have out and ready, which rods I am going to use, and how we are going to set up the bait and rigs. Other questions I consider: Have people been getting hammered by blue sharks in the area lately? If the water is cooler, blue sharks will most likely show up. Will I be able to sight fish?

After you get your operation set in your mind, get the appropriate rods and leaders out. (See "Rods and Reels" for configurations). If they haven't been prepared prior to leaving harbor, do so now by tying swivels to the lines. The next step is to sharpen your hooks, even if you think they don't need sharpening. Once that's done, get out appropriate bait to match your hook sizes.

> TIP: If you want to be eligible for IGFA records, don't go longer than 30 feet on your leader or exceed a 130 pound test line on your reel. Refer to the IGFA website at www.igfa.org for a complete list of rules.

The Spread

In previous chapters, we talked about preparing bait and chum for when you get out in the water. I like to take out a dozen thawed whole mackerel, a couple thawed tuna (maybe used for side slabs, heads, fillets, etc.), and giant squid (if available) for rigging bait. Your bait should be thawed, as working with frozen bait is extremely difficult.

Bait Configurations and Presentation

A configuration of multiple bait types should be ready for use at all times. If you are going to put bait in the water while you are drifting, you should have one, two, or three different bait configurations at any given time. The best spread, giving you optimum water coverage with minimal gear, is a three-bait configuration, or as I like to call it, the 1-2-3 spread. Regardless of the bait configuration I use, I keep a shotgun rig ready.

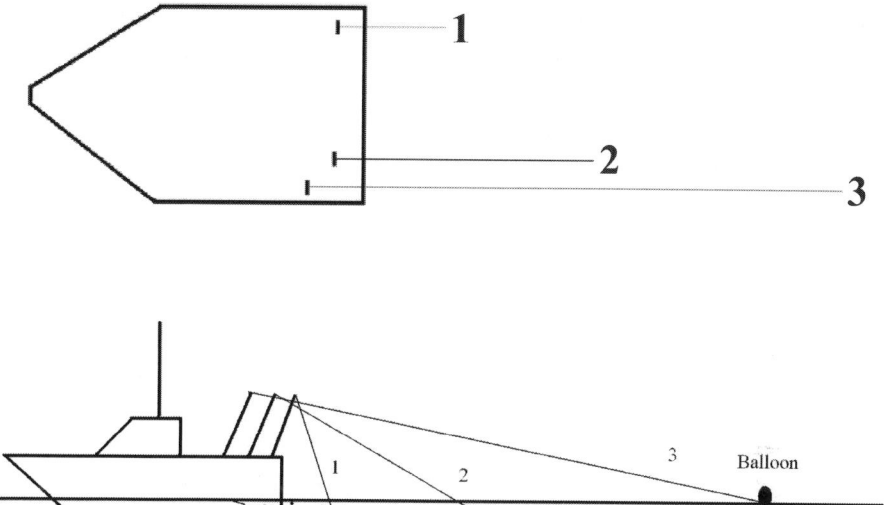

Chum Line
Keep your bait within the chum line covering the different depths. Always try to maintain minimum line slack and avoid excessive line twist.

Shotgun Rig
The shotgun rig is a rod and reel that has been rigged with a wire leader, that is ready to cast on an already-sighted fish and can be baited quickly. Refer to the shotgun rig setups in the *Rods and Reels* chapter for equipment details and specifications.

Setting up Bait Configurations and Presentation
These are the configurations I like to use. For more detail and specifics about the equipment, refer to *Drift Bait* in the Rods and Reels chapter.

Rod 1 - short range: I keep an 80 pound outfit near the back of the boat (baited with a slab or belly) with the swivel just touching the surface, down about 15 feet with a 15 foot leader on it (with a 400-600 pound test wire).

Rod 2 - mid-range: I keep another 80 pound outfit (baited with a large, whole mackerel or a very small bullet tuna) about 20 yards out, 20 feet down, with a 20-25 foot leader on it (with a 600-800 pound test wire).

Rod 3 - Long range: I keep an 80 or 130 pound outfit (baited with a large tuna head with plenty of belly on it, or a whole tuna) 40 yards out, 28 feet down, with a 30 foot leader on it (with an 80 pound test wire). I like to keep a balloon attached 1 foot below the swivel on the wire leader. It is important to keep the balloon on the leader so that your line doesn't get bit through by a shark. On a slow drift day, you may want to use a balloon on your second line as well. On a fast drift a balloon might not be needed at all.

> NOTE: Once the spread is out, get that tag stick out and ready!

Setting the Reels for a Blind Strike and Hit

1. Once your lines are out in the water (assuming you've already done your presets on your drags), set the strike on your reels as loose as possible, basically a free spool situation with the clicker on. If you set your reels this way, when a fish picks up your bait and starts to run with it, there will be no tension on the line. You don't want your line too loose, though, because if a speeding Mako crashes on your bait, he could take off at a high rate of speed, causing a backlash on your reel before you can get to it.
2. Get your Mako Magnet out in the water and turn it on.
3. Whenever possible, I like to check to see if I can see my bait in the water. You need to see if a shark is moving in on your bait. Know where your bait is at all times.
4. Check drift again, making sure everything is good and you're on course. Make minor adjustments to the wheel if necessary.
5. Next, prepare your fly gaffs by tying them off. Sharpen them if necessary.

6. Have someone keep an eye on the rods and scan the water at all times.
7. During the setup process, if you come across any bad gear or rusted hooks, set them aside for replacement. If gear or hooks look iffy, they probably are. Don't use them, and always replace any damaged equipment. You're not dealing with your average fish, and the reliability and strength of your gear will determine whether or not you make that catch.

Hooking & Fighting Sharks; Boating the Mako

You're out on the water. You've found your grounds, put your bait in the water, and are anxiously waiting for a strike from your intended quarry, a Mako shark. The adventure is just beginning.

Hooking a Mako involves much more than getting a shark to swim up and grab a chunk of meat off a baited hook. Some serious trickery is involved. You've scented the water to lure the Mako to the boat but getting it to eat a baited hook on a wire leader isn't exactly easy. You must convince the Mako that it's going to get the right kind of meal. You can do this by making a dead bait look alive, or by offering a slab bait that is consistent with its regular diet. If you miss it the first time, you probably won't see it again.

Once you lure the Mako into taking your bait then set the hook, the battle begins. Everything you've learned is for this moment of truth. You've got an enraged shark connected to you, fighting for its life. You have to catch the insane beast on an 80-pound line that must hold without breaking. As if that's not enough, you need to get it to your boat without letting it take a chunk out of you, your crew or your vessel. You must subdue the monster and bring it in, or remove your hook and release it.

The Crew

Now that you're set up and waiting for the shark to show, take a few moments to reflect the condition of the boat, where the equipment is, and who is going to do what and when. Even though I have fished for sharks on several occasions by myself or with only one other person, I recommend a four-man crew for big game fishing. Each person has an assigned duty. Typical duty assignments are:

1. Rod man
2. Leader man
3. Gaff man
4. Driver (of the boat)

Delegating and Multi-tasking

Although the captain may want to (or feel he has to) do everything himself, it's best to delegate and spread the work out. Teamwork is crucial to a successful mission. Every crew member will have multiple duties that must be performed at a particular time, and you may need to switch up at a moment's notice. For example, if you have a regular wireman and he happens to be on the rod when you need wiring, you will need to know who is your next best wire man.

Duties on a sharking expedition are not constant. At one point in the trip, a duty will be necessary, and later it won't. For example, when you have a fish hooked, you won't need a chum man; you'll begin chunking at this point. The dual duties below work well for most people.

1. Rod man - begins the expedition on lookout, or as watchman of the rods
2. Leader man - begins the expedition cutting bait and working the chum barrel
3. Gaff man - begins the expedition in the tower sight fishing with binoculars
4. Driver - puts the motors in forward upon a strike and oversees everything at the helm, usually the captain.

You should take some time thinking about crew assignments. When assigning duties, always consider who is best suited for each one based on physical abilities, mental awareness, and fear factor.

Keeping Your Percentages Up

In one tournament we had 20 or so miles of ocean to cross. I had my best spotter eyeballing the water on the way out. I chose my rod man based on his ability to cast a shotgun rig. I was at the helm because I had the most experience with the boat. In this particular tournament, there were five of us on the boat. I made my decisions based on winning the tournament and keeping the percentages up on who was best qualified for what duty. My spotter is capable of spotting any fin that comes our way, and is able to distinguish shark fins from every type of aquatic life. This saves me time from stopping the boat constantly. My rod man has the knowledge of the workings of the equipment and casting and fighting of these fish. I was behind the wheel because I know the vessel and how to position it like the back of my hand. Being a tournament situation and having no room for error, I had to pick the best and only the best and we prevailed. When the spotter sighted a finning Mako, I called the rod man, who was down below catching some early morning Z's on the way out. He flew out of the cabin wielding a shotgun rig, baited it right away, and got a fix on the shark. Meanwhile, I positioned the boat to drag the bait just in front of the swimming shark, so the shark would not be spooked by the boat or motors, and so at the proper moment, the shark and bait would meet. This allowed the rod man to get the right cast. The rod man made the cast and we dragged the bait just across the shark's nose. Sure enough, we got picked up and the hook was set. The battle was on!

We did not have to make repeated passes or multiple attempts to snag this Mako. The shark didn't sink on us, leaving us waiting and hoping he would come back up. By choosing the best man for each job and preparing ourselves, we succeeded on the first try.

On a non-tournament fishing day, you might relax a bit on your duty assignments because everybody is anxious to hook and fight a big fish. Someone other than your first choice of rod man, the leader man for example, may pick up a rod and set the hook. Is the new rod man knowledgeable and capable enough to handle fighting this large fish? Is someone available to take over the leader man's job? As anxious and excited as your crew may be to hook a fish, remember you spent a lot of time, money, and resources on this trip, and you don't want to lose a big fish due to an inexperienced angler or his lack of knowledge of the equipment. If you're going to switch duties around, don't put anyone in a position in which they feel uncomfortable or unsafe. Experiment with duty assignments; shuffle and rearrange them until you get the right mix.

A Small Shark is Sighted

The majority of your catches are going to be in the 100 pound and under class. Even though you're baited up for medium to monster size fish, the one thing you don't want to do is hook a small fish with a

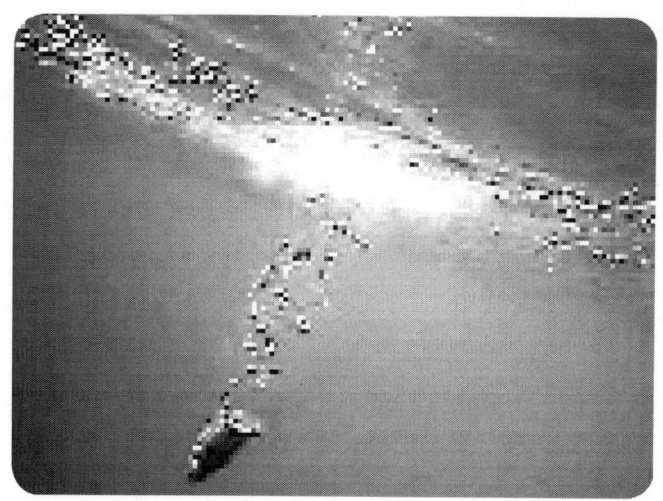

gigantic hook. Not only is it unsporting, it could injure the creature and cost you some gear. If you can eyeball it, try to determine the species and size the fish. If you can see the shark's fin and tail as it swims by or crashes the balloon, you'll get an idea as to the size of the fish. Knowing what you're dealing with will save you a lot of time, energy, and equipment.

If it's a small fish, lure it to the boat by reeling in your large bait and throwing out a small baited shotgun rig to the fish. Eventually switch to a smaller hook and bait size. You don't want to hook a small Mako with monster sized bait; the shark will only mutilate the bait, rendering it unusable. When a small Mako is hooked, you might choose to leave out another rod. If you do, keep that rod out of the way as much as possible so you won't get your lines crossed. While you're playing with the smaller Mako, a large one may grab your other hook. I've seen Makos travel in pairs, and when they are in the 100 pound class, they are often carbon copies of each other. Either way, prepare yourself for a double hook.

Blue sharks will often swim past your bait, right up to the boat, the source of your chum. If they do, keep them away from your baited hooks. Keep them interested at the stern of the boat by feeding them little chunks. It is most important to keep them away from the lines. If you need to, put your baited hooks farther out so they are even farther from the boat. If at any point you see the blue sharks leave, there's a good chance a Mako is near, so be ready.

Is the Fish Eating or Investigating/Scouting?

If a fish appears to be investigating the area in which you've set up, get it to eat by throwing bait chunks to it. If the fish doesn't take your bait, try a different type of bait, as sometimes a Mako won't want what you're presenting. Only throw small amounts — you're trying to attract the shark, not feed it dinner. If that fails, you can make your dead bait appear live by popping the line to make your bait jump. I catch most of my finicky sharks by popping the line.

Designate one guy to be the lookout man. He should watch the water, line, and rod tips. He should simultaneously listen for the clicker. The lookout's position on the boat is one of the most important positions. Give your lookout man the best seat on the boat, one where he can easily see the rods. If your boat has a tower, that's the ideal location for your lookout. It's not always easy to notice when a fish has hit your line. Look out for these scenarios:

- Bait gets bumped and the clicker clicks only once or twice
- Rod tip bounces ever so slightly
- Balloon jolts or bounces rapidly
- You see the fish (or a dark shadow) for a split second
- Your bait gets grabbed and hauled off at a high rate. This one's easy to spot.

My experience has taught me that when the rod gets bumped causing the clicker on the reel to click once or twice, or the rod tip bounces slightly, that I've been bumped by a shark. When this happens I immediately grab the rod and reel and prepare myself for the monster to come back and grab the bait before going on its run. Every time it happens, I remember the scene in the movie Jaws when Quint is sitting in the fighting chair and the reel clicks twice. He straps himself to the rod and prepares for the run off while the crew has no idea what's happening. This often happens to me. When I tell my crew that I'm getting hit they ask me how I know, as if I'm crazy. "I didn't see or hear anything," they say. Then suddenly the clicker starts screaming on the reel as the line peels off.

It's like a game of chess. Your opponent makes his move and you respond with yours. Like any other game, it's not exciting unless you're in the game. Getting into shark fishing includes being able to spot and predict your opponent's moves. When your calls and predictions are successful, it's very rewarding.

The Shark Took the Bait, Now What Do I Do?

Right now you should have three rods out in the water: a short-range, mid-range, and long-range. Hopefully your shotgun rig is ready, too. Recall the 1-2-3 spread we discussed in the previous chapter. Let's break these up now into two groups: short group and long group. The short group consists of the short-range rod and shotgun rig, and the long group includes the mid-range and long-range rod.

The rod on which the shark is feeding or hooked determines your reaction. If it's feeding on a rod from the long group, you won't be able to see if the bait is completely in the shark's mouth (because it is so far away). You will need to wait until the bait is in its mouth before setting the hook, be patient count to seven and then set the hook. If it's hooked on a rod from the short group, you will be able to see the bait clearly and you will have more control.

Reaction Examples
1. Long group

I've noticed sharks going for the bait many times from just the rod tip bouncing slightly, a couple of clicks off the spool, a bob of the balloon, or a quick glimpse of a darting shark. When this happens I jump up from my seat and grab the rod, making sure it's set in 100% free spool and the rod tip is pointed in the same direction as the line (giving minimum resistance on the line). Then I wait to be picked up. When you are picked up, let the shark take the initial run, usually 10 to 30 yards. When he stops, this means he's putting the bait in his mouth. Don't set the hook just yet. Wait for him to run again, so the bait is firmly planted in his mouth. Then go into strike position and reel down all the slack until you feel the weight of the shark pulling the line. When everything goes tight, you can set the hook.

2. Short group

Once the shark picks up the bait and you can visibly see that the shark has the bait firmly in its mouth, wait for it to turn its head and swim away from the boat before setting the hook. Otherwise, the shark could go ballistic and jump straight *into* the boat. The main reason to wait until the sharks is swimming away from the boat is to prevent yourself from pulling the bait and hook straight out of the shark's mouth. You'll get a better hook set in the corner of the shark's mouth when he's swimming away or off to the side.

Setting the Hook

Before setting the hook, reel all your line taut and put your reel in the strike position. Sometimes your strike position might not have enough pounds of pressure on the drag to get a good hook set. In this case simply hold the spool with your thumb to keep the line from going out upon the hook set. Setting the hook requires three or four solid jerks on the rod. Each time you jerk the rod, make sure the line is taught and there's no slack. Remember that monofilament line has stretch (as opposed to Dacron's inflexibility) making setting the hook harder. Once you do set the hook, prepare for the shark to explode. If this happens, back off on the drag a little (if necessary) to let the shark make its 30-plus mile per hour run.

CAUTION: When the shark is running, don't get your finger caught in between the spooled line and the reel plate.

When you set your hook, the Mako may come to or attack the boat, though this is a very rare occurrence. If a Mako comes to one side of the boat, be prepared for him to dart under the boat and go to the other side. If you can anticipate this, quickly head toward the other side of the boat before the Mako to keep your line from sawing off. You won't be able to pass the line behind the back of the boat (due to the motors and the rudders), so you have to go around the bow. If the fish is very large, start the motors and move the boat away from the fish.

Jaw Set or Gut Set

There are two primary types of hook sets -- jaw sets and gut sets. In the gut set, the shark swallows the bait and the hook as well. This is not something you want to happen. Not only can it severely hurt the fish, making it impossible to release (as it will most likely die), but the fight is not as sporting. In the jaw set, you set the hook in the shark's jaw as quick as possible, which is especially ideal for tag and release. A jaw set's going to give you the most spectacular fight from the fish, prevent internal injury of the fish, allow it to run quickly, give you an acrobatic show that will blow you away, make leading the fish easier, and allow you to easily remove the hook for tag and release. It also results in less lost gear and ensures a higher survival rate for the shark. As you get more and more involved in the sport, you'll find yourself getting better in the technique and safely releasing more and more sharks without ever losing a hook.

> TIP: As often as you can, use light gear, wires, and short leaders for tag and release, as it increases the chance of survival for the tagged and released fish.

Save Those Hooks!

One of the reasons I like to sight fish is because it allows me to bait the fish at the back of the boat and get a quicker hook set on the fish. These are always my more rewarding catches. It was something that I had to teach myself, as I was always taught blind fishing by others. It took me several years to learn and perfect sight fishing with the type of gear I use today. Perhaps the biggest advantage is that it gives me the option of choosing what fish I want to hook with what gear.

Unlike with blind fishing, I don't have to deal with tangled gear or releasing fish I don't want to hook (which could prevent me from getting a nicer fish). By now you're probably wondering why I spent all this time talking about the short and long range rods if I'm just going to be sight fishing. Remember you can only sight fish if water and sky conditions permit (see "Finding Shark Grounds"). When I am sight fishing, I keep two or three baited shotgun rigs out and ready for use, out of the water. Most of my catches are done with these (group one from "Rods and Reels"). Since the shark is near the boat and you're using a shotgun rig, it's easy to set the hook because you don't have extra line and long distances to worry about. It also causes less damage to the fish because you are able to get a quick hook set.

When I first got into shark fishing, I used to lose an average of five hooks a day for various reasons — blue sharks, gut hooks, getting busted off by big Makos, etc. Now I rarely lose five hooks in a season because of these improved techniques. At $5 - $30 a rig, you can see how quickly the expenses can add up, so you'll want to improve your technique as fast as you can, for your wallet's sake and for the shark's health.

It's Hooked, Now What?

Wait, no it's not! If the shark spits the hook, assume the shark will come back. Leave your bait out. If you have another rod with a fresh bait ready, get it out as quick as possible to replace the one with mutilated bait. Though the chances of that shark coming back are slim, it never hurts to try. Typically a spooked Mako will run away, but if it's aggressive or hungry enough there's no stopping it from coming back and picking up the line again.

Ok, now it's hooked. Clear the deck! Slimy bait lying around, buckets, extra equipment you don't need, and people standing in the rod man's way can only lead to disaster. Keep roaming space available; you're going to be doing a lot of moving around the boat. Have one guy put a fighting belt on the rod man. Have someone else put away the excess rods and pull any gear out of the water.

Maintaining the Line and Drag

While Mono line has a good stretch and is harder to break, it can easily chafe and create weak points. Dacron, having no stretch, requires you to maintain your drag sensitivity in comparison with the speed of the shark. On initial high speed runs and when a Mako is close to the boat, be prepared to back off on the drag as the Mako makes short bursts away from the boat. While fighting a monster fish, making minor adjustments to your drag settings will be necessary at different times during the fight. At certain points in a fight, I might want minimal stretch and drag to put as much pressure on the fish as possible. If the fish decides to take a run or make a jump, I will quickly back off on the drag. It can take anywhere from one to half a dozen quick, consecutive back-to-back jumps. This would require a lot of line to be fed out in a very short amount of time.

Fish On

As the fish runs away from the boat it distances itself from you, up to a couple hundred yards in some cases. In addition to that, you have other forces working against you, such as the line drag in the water. Just a quick note: just because your line goes slack, it doesn't mean you've lost your shark. You might have this happen and put the rod on the rod holder in disgust only to find the line go tight again. *Always* assume you are still hooked up no matter what and reel as fast

as you can. Reel, reel, reel! You might find the shark is coming toward the boat. You'll want to take up all that slack as fast as possible, or the shark may very easily chew your line off.

If you hook a large fish, you're probably going to be in for a ride, so get those motors ready to chase it. Whoever is at the helm needs to be aware of which way the fish is swimming and where the line is at all times. If you're hooked onto a small fish (100 pounds or under) you don't need to worry about starting the motors, you can fight it without moving the boat.

If you're going to back the boat down on the fish and are using a fighting chair, get someone to maneuver the man in the fighting chair into the proper position (determined by which way the line is going). On the west coast, fishing is typically done in stand-up gear. We are able to go to the bow of the boat when necessary to chase the fish and come back to the stern. If you have the proper harnesses, it makes a stand-up fight much easier. I chased a large fish once for seven nautical miles in four hours. Backing down on that fish was definitely not an option.

A lot of times big game fish will sound. To get them to the surface, move the boat forward, always staying ahead of the fish and going in the same direction as it is swimming. Gradually crank the fish and pull him to the surface. This is known as planing the fish. Once the shark is up it will usually stay there. It can be tricky, though, as they often dart from one side of the boat to the other. If they are sounding and darting, be careful at the back of the boat because your line will be pretty much straight down and could hit the props.

Always remember that anything can happen at any time. Be prepared for whatever could happen, because it probably will. Don't rule any possibilities out, from being almost pulled overboard to the shark jumping in your boat.

TIP: Keep one hand for the boat and one hand for yourself.

Playing the Mako

One of the most exciting things to see is a larger than life shark jumping around in the water. People can teach dolphins to do it, so why not a Mako? I call this training your Mako. Ok, so it's not exactly the same as teaching a dolphin to jump but by mastering some techniques you can have your hooked Mako put on an acrobatic show for you and your guests, on your command. Be sure to have your cameras rolling! Hopefully, sooner than later on in your Mako fishing experiences, you'll find yourself using your camera more than your gaff.

> CAMERA TIP: The most important thing when taking a picture or filming a video is to not be a slave to your camera. Your boat is going to be swaying side to side no matter how calm the water is, trying to film through a viewfinder or take a picture through a small hole is incredibly difficult. Use your eyes to focus on where the fish is or where you presume it is and point your camera in that direction. Be prepared for that split-second shot when that fish goes airborne.

Techniques for Training the Mako

The best way to train a Mako is to get a quick jaw set so you're able to lead the fish around and gain better control of it. Granted, if you hook a monster it's going to do whatever it wants and your only real option is to hang on. But if you hook a smaller fish and you can use some *really* light gear, you can have a lot of fun with a 40 to 150 pound fish. Once you've insured you have a good hook set, get ready because this is when the shark is the most aggressive and has the most energy. Let it think it's getting away and leave the rod and reel in free spool with the clicker on. Keep very light thumb pressure so you don't get any backlash. If the Mako doesn't jump after the count of five, stop the Mako in its tracks with a quick jolt. Apply thumb pressure to the spool to keep the line from going out and pull up on the rod slightly. Then let the line go out again, and let it run. I can almost guarantee the Mako will pop out of the water to try and throw out the hook. Usually they will jump two to three times, but I've trained Makos to do an average of six jumps. This is what I call "fly the kite." We've captured some great film footage of airborne sharks using these methods.

"Fly the kite" is the process of getting a Mako to go airborne. Usually it does a back flip with a twist, as high as fifteen feet in the air. They seem to be able to flip consecutively in a matter of seconds. It's an awesome sight and one of the most spectacular things I've ever seen on the water. It's adrenaline-rushing, heart-pumping material for sure.

When you're done training your Mako and having fun with it, you are ready for release. Bring it to the boat, look it in the eye and let it know who's boss. Then set the Mako free to fight again another day. Try and enjoy the fish and have some fun, and don't think you have to kill a Mako to remember it. Moment's like this you'll never forget. I still remember my first one.

No Two Makos are Alike

All Makos are different. From their shape and size to their attitude, no two Makos are completely alike. Some are curious, some are docile. Other sharks are skittish, calm, or aggressive. A calm shark that swims right up to the boat can turn aggressive once you stick a gaff in it. You *never* know what to expect. That's why there's no such thing as a typical fight. That doesn't mean you can't prepare yourself, but don't rely solely on your predictions.

Tiring a Mako

To ensure the easiest (not to mention safest) fight, tire out your Mako before bringing it to the boat. In my opinion, the most dangerous fight is with a calm Mako. A calm Mako is conserving its energy, and like a time bomb is ready to explode that second you gaff it (at which point it *should* be tired already). Make an extra effort to tire out a Mako that remains calm when hooked.

The best thing to do is stay ahead of the Mako, keeping it at an angle to the stern. Try to keep the rod man at the stern of the boat. If the rod man is at the bow, get him over to the stern by positioning the boat on one side of the shark and maneuvering yourself ahead of the shark. Meanwhile, the rod man can work his way toward the stern. Staying ahead of the fish rather than chasing it ensures the leader be out in front of the fish. If you're chasing the fish, you risk the leader wrapping against the Mako's body or tail, which could very easily cut the fishing line.

Stay ahead of the Mako, but point your boat in the same direction the fish is traveling. It's not uncommon for a Mako to pick a direction and stick to it. I have tried to force a big fish into another direction but was unsuccessful, but that's not to say it's impossible.

Whether it's you leading the fish or the fish taking control of you, as long as you are moving the boat with the fish, you're in good shape. It is easier to fight the fish by traveling in the same direction as it than it is to fight it dead in the water. You should now be ready to plane the fish and work it to the side of the boat. With the leader in front of the fish as you gradually pull the fish to the boat, you've set yourself up ideally to leader it. This method generally results in a more calm reaction from the fish.

> *Note: Sharks can drown. IF the fish leads you, he might wrap himself in the leader and drown. If this happens you may lose the fish and kill it.*

> *SAFTEY TIP: If you're clipped to a fighting belt, unclip the belt when going to and from the bow so you don't get pulled overboard.*

Leadering the Fish

Here's where gut instinct needs to come into play. Do you ever get that feeling that you should be doing something differently from the way you're doing it? Well you'll be getting a lot of that out in the water for sure. Usually your first instinct is correct, so keep this in mind as the Mako comes alongside the boat. If anything seems wrong or odd, a red flag should go up. Immediately reevaluate the situation. If at any point you find yourself wishing you had done something differently, you probably knew in the back of your head that you should have but decided against it. Once the bullet leaves the barrel, it's not going back in, no matter how badly you want it. So if you ever get in such a situation, don't be surprised if your next action is calling the Coast Guard for an emergency.

Don't get me wrong, you're going to have a weird feeling regardless when you're subduing or slaying a monster. I keep saying in the book that no matter how much you prepare yourself for a trip, something, no matter how slight, will go wrong. I may say it a lot but I can't emphasize it enough. Particularly right now, as this section is the most dangerous and most likely something will go wrong.

By now the captain must have made an important decision: what will be the fate of the Mako? Are you tagging or releasing the fish to be fought another day? Or having it for dinner? Either way, it's time to leader the fish. During this process it's critical the captain remain in charge.

If you've chosen to tag or release the fish, refer to the *Tagging and Releasing Sharks* chapter. If you're gaffing the fish read on ahead.

So what's happening right now? The boat should be moving forward and the rod man should be at the stern fighting the fish, but not for long. He needs to make way for the leader man and gaff man by moving forward, toward the bow in the cockpit area. At this point, the rod man should unclip himself if he's in a harness.

The leader man needs to have his gloves on and get to the side of the boat. The gaff man (who I recommend wears wiring gloves) moves into position at the back of the boat, with the leader man in between the rod and gaff man. Note that everyone should be on the same side of the boat.

The rod man needs to prepare the reel by backing off on the drag as soon as the wire man grabs a hold of the leader, just in case the shark decides to take a run. More often than not, a Mako will go ballistic once you try and gaff it. That's why Makos are so dangerous to gaff and you need to be particularly cautious.

With his wiring gloves equipped, the leader man grabs the leader and pulls the beast toward him. The Makos head should be facing the bow of boat with the tail pointing at the stern. Of course the boat should be in forward motion and the fish along the side.

Pulling the Wire

The leader man reaches out and takes a wrap on the leader with one hand and grabs the leader with the other, pulling the fish alongside the boat.

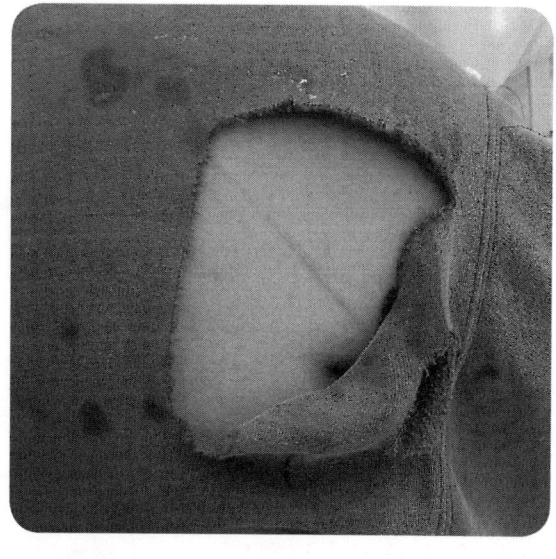

One time on a trip out, one of my crew men was passing a wire leader over his shoulder while pulling a shark in, so the coil lay behind him. When the shark took off, he couldn't hold it and had to let go of the leader. The leader passed back over his shoulder cutting through his shirt and part of his shoulder. Luckily nothing severe happened, but the accident could have been a lot worse. He could have easily avoided the accident though had he pulled the leader off to the side rather than behind him.

If the Mako didn't bolt after being brought alongside the boat, it's time for the gaff man to gaff it. With the tied off fly gaff, bury the hook just behind the dorsal fin in the back of the shark. The captain should stop the boat immediately. If the gaff man succeeded in getting a good sink on the gaff, the shark is going to bolt and the gaff rope line will feed out fast. Don't even try to hold the rope on a big shark unless you enjoy rope burn. The leader man might need to dump the leader and the rod man may need to go back into a fighting prone position, just in case the gaff comes out of the shark. Let the leader go only if you can't hold it.

If the gaff man didn't get a good sink of the gaff or barely poked the Mako, it could still go ballistic. Heck it happens quite often. The wire man better dump the fish right away by freeing the wire from his hands and moving out of the way along with the gaff man. The rod man comes back into rod position at the stern. A good captain would be moving the boat forward and away from the fish at this point. Now you could potentially be in for another couple hours fight before getting another chance to leader the fish.

If your gaff was successful, the gaff man should pull on the rope line and the leader man get the leader back into his hands if he did dump it. He may need to call on the rod man for help. The captain can leave the helm finally and stick a second gaff in the front of the shark. Now whoever is capable should tie a tail rope around the tail of the Mako and cleat it off. The person who does this should take notice that the shark could go crazy at this point. So this guy needs to be able to deal with a flipping tail and jerking body. Rest assured that once the tail rope is on the shark is not going anywhere now. Don't confuse that with it not being a threat anymore.

Make sure the shark is very well stretched out alongside the boat and secured because it's time to tie a head rope. You need a head rope and a tail rope because you can't depend on the gaffs staying in place. On many occasions I've had them pop out; it's just not worth taking that risk without reinforcements. Get out your hunting knife (I use my Ka-Bar) and cut the gills to bleed it out.

This scenario may sound easy to some of you, but its hard work, incredibly dangerous, and in most cases at gaff is when the fish is lost. A fight or two will tell you soon enough where you're lacking in equipment or ability to subdue such a sea monster.

Here are a few of the countless possible outcomes while fighting a Mako, so remember something probably will go wrong on every trip, no matter how minor:

- Your fly gaff straightens out pulling clean out of a shark, resulting in a lost shark.
- Having a shark bite off a piece of your boat.
- A Mako pulling a rod or reel out of your hands and busting up your gear.
- A Mako rolling in the rope and ending up in the cockpit area.
- A Mako jumping into the boat.
- Getting blood drawn from yourself or one of your mates. There are many dangerous and hazardous items on your boat, not even to mention the hundreds of teeth of a shark.

At the end of the trip, record *everything* into your log book: where you hooked up, how long the fight was, how far the fish drove you, the people who were with you, water temperature, sea conditions, and anything else you can think of. Don't forget to measure your shark on the girth and fork length.

Tagging & Releasing Sharks

This photo should be imprinted into your brain. Why you ask? Even though this book is about shark fishing you should think about the final outcome once you do catch one I recommend practicing CFR, Catch, Film, and Release.

Upon arriving at my fishing spot, one of the first things I do is set a tag into a tag stick, high and out of the way in a rocket launcher, ready to use at any time. I prepare my stick early because it gives me peace of mind. I know if I have my tag stick ready to go I don't have to think about it until it is time to use it. After the stick is prepared and stowed above, I am ready for whatever comes my way. Preparing a tag stick feels better to me than preparing all the other equipment on my boat. I'd rather have a tag stick prepared than a fly gaff. To me, the tag stick is the more important tool. On several occasions, I've tagged a free-swimming shark without ever having to set a hook, because the tag stick was prepared and ready to use.

Tagging and releasing should be at the top of your mind of when you do get a shark to the boat. The shark population today is declining, so I release most of my catches. I *catch, film and release* (CFR) 99% of the time.

Here on the west cost we are allowed to keep two Makos per angler, per day. If you have five anglers on the boat, you can keep ten Makos. I think it should be lowered to two per boat, per day (or even one), at least until the shark population rebounds. With the finning of sharks around the world still in full swing, I don't see this happening anytime soon. As sportsmen, we must fish responsibly and overcome the urge to kill every fish that swims our way.

I have tagged many sharks and have also retrieved tags from sharks in the Pacific Ocean. The tags were sent to the U.S. Department of Fish and Game (USDFG); they use the tags they receive to track the fish and store the data. Assisting the USDFG is both fun and rewarding. They sent me an official Tag & Release hat along with the information about the sharks I captured — where the shark was tagged, how long it was at liberty, how much more it grew and the routes it swam. Some tags that have been returned provided information showing routes of over 3,000 miles swam by some tagged sharks. I have also tagged many juvenile white sharks in the Santa Monica Bay with archival satellite pop up tags.

Tag and release shark tournaments are a good way to introduce the tagging program and to promote the releasing of fish (as opposed to "kill and take it to the scales" type tournaments). Some shark tournaments require the kill of a prize-winning shark to place in the tournament. The captured sharks are only degraded after weigh-in. This is not responsible fishing as it is counterproductive to shark stocks.

I also teach tag and release to the kids. It is a great way to get the younger generation into this sport and to teach the kids conservation.

As you hone your sharking fishing skills you will find catch and release fishing easy and fulfilling. Don't forget to take plenty of videos and photos! Sharks are magnificent animals. These top predators bring true exhilaration and compassion to my heart. I hope you fall in love with this sport, and like me, want the sharks to be here for your sons and daughters to enjoy. This section explains the proper procedures on how to do a proper tag and release.

Tagging Procedure
1. Use minimal size hook and wire lengths when fishing for sharks so they will have a higher survival rate. Always use non-stainless steel hooks because they will rust out and increase the shark's survival chances.
2. Try to get the fish to swim toward the bow of the ship. Pulling the wire or using a rod is usually the best method. Move the boat forward if necessary on larger fish. Use your basic leadering procedures to bring the fish alongside the boat. (Refer to *Hooking and Fighting Sharks* for more information on leadering).
3. As the wire man or rod man steps out of the way, the tagging man should step in with the stick as the shark swims a few feet from the boat.
4. The tag man should thrust the shark with tag stick. Tags should be inserted at the base of the dorsal fin. Do not pierce through the fin itself.
5. As the tag man steps back, the rod man should move back into his former position. The rod man should be prepared for the fish to jolt and make a run.
6. The tag man should put the tag stick away and get the release stick out.
7. The rod man and wire man should bring the fish alongside the boat.
8. Gather the appropriate information and fill out the tag card. For length, either guess or physically measure. If you can't get this information or guess it, it is best to leave it blank. If the shark is too big or you can't get all the information, just release it. Better safe than sorry. Even if a card isn't 100% complete, it is still useful.
9. Once you have gotten the information, release the shark.

NOTE: *Latitude, longitude, female or male and type of shark are the most important pieces of information. Don't worry if you can't get the rest.*

Tagging a shark

Boat Side

Even smaller sharks in the 200 to 300 pound range can pull you overboard. Every shark has a distinctive appearance and a unique fight. Sometimes sharks act as if they don't know they are hooked, but when you bring them alongside the boat, they remember. Oh yeah, they seem to think, this is not right, and then they come alive, fighting like lunatics. The shark might take a bite out of your boat or make a run for it with all the energy that it didn't waste when you were fighting it. This is a very explosive and dangerous scenario that happens far too often to the careless, overconfident and inexperienced.

I experienced such an explosive situation. One day I made the mistake of being a little overconfident, thinking I could hold the leader on a shark to do to a quick release. It was a small shark, in the 200 to 300 pound range. This shark was brought to the boat too quickly — it did not fight very hard until we brought it to the boat. Then, all hell broke loose. That insane shark was exploding at the side of my boat while I was holding the wire leader with all my might and hoping it would simmer down. The rod man put the rod in the rod holder to see if he could help. Big mistake! Right then, complete with the thrashing wire and the shark, the wire leader took a couple of wraps around the fishing pole. It was a $450 pole with a $800 reel on it. I freaked, knowing I could not hold the shark and I did not have even a second to spare to unwind the leader from the fishing pole. The shark was just about to pull me overboard, so I let go, fully aware that the fishing pole was going to take the full brunt of this shark going crazy at boat side. When the shark took off, the wire leader went tight and the rod bent over. I stepped back and watched the wire leader strip the roller guides off the rod. I expected the worse but was lucky. All that was damaged was the one rod. It was going to the repair shop. It could have been much worse if I, or a fellow angler, had been caught in the wire leader.

Sharks, fierce, apex predators, must be respected on all levels. Here are a couple of other things to remember when getting close to these critters at boat side. One, sharks can contort their bodies and bend all the way around; they can bite their own tail. Two, they can easily roll up in the wire leader cinching everything (gaffs, fishing poles, fingers, ropes) down against their bodies.

Releasing Procedure
1. You should only use release stick if the hook is in the shark's jaw or mouth.
2. Use your basic leadering procedures to bring the fish alongside the boat. (Refer to *Hooking and Fighting Sharks* for more information on leadering.)
3. The wire leader needs to be held taut. The release stick is clipped on the wire leader, passing it down the wire leader to the shank of the hook.
4. At this point, the wire leader and release stick should both have pressure on them with no slack whatsoever.
5. If the hook is on the outside of the jaw, give the wire leader a little slack and at the same time do a pushing/popping motion downward to pop the hook out of the shark's jaw.

6. If the hook is inside the jaw, follow the previous step but pull back on the wire as fast as possible to cinch it back tight with the release stick.
7. If you can't use a release stick, use bolt cutters to cut the hook or at the least use wire cutters to cut the wire leader as close as possible to the hook. Always put your own safety before the sharks!

Personal Opinion

While I believe strongly in both government and private tagging programs, I don't tag every fish that swims alongside my boat. I try to tag at least one shark per fishing day. Considering that the metal tip of the tag (the part inserted into the shark) is 1 ¼" long, I choose not to tag any shark that is smaller than four feet.

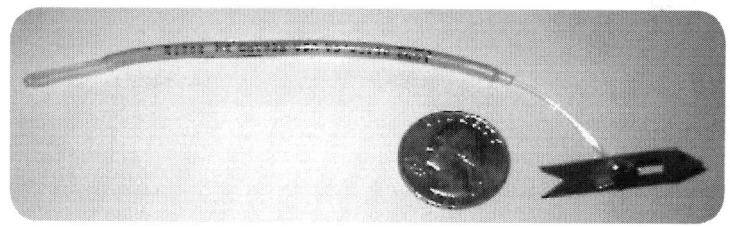

Tag: The metal tip is inserted into the shark, which you can see is not much larger than a quarter.

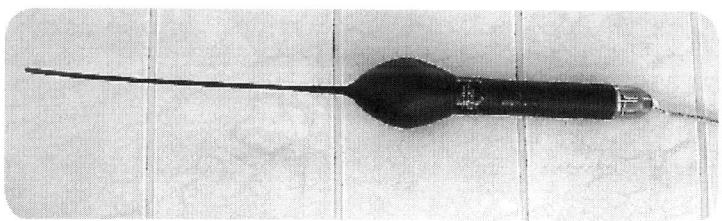

Satellite Tags

Satellite tags are currently used by marine biologists for tagging white sharks, Makos, and a few other species. Tags are set for a predetermined release time, typically 90 days before they pop off and float to the surface. These tags are used to record travel patterns and speed, water temperatures, depths, and the number of tail flicks a shark takes to propel itself through the water. Given the cost of producing these, they are not commonly used. As technology improves and costs drop, I hope that all shark fishermen will be able to have access to satellite tags.

As much as I appreciate the tagging program, I do fear the information being gathered might get into the wrong hands. As it is right now, commercial shark fishing is out of control. If commercial boat fleets were to obtain this information, given their technology and resources, there is the possibility of greatly reducing the shark stocks with pinpoint accuracy.

Butchering the Mako

Like all other hunted animals, you should not kill Makos if you don't plan to make proper use of their meat. These very tasty fish make a healthy addition to your diet. They can be cooked and served in a variety of ways. The meat can also be frozen for later use.

Makos play a very important role in our ecosystem, and should not be wasted. If you don't plan to eat your catches yourself, there are many places where you can donate the meat. Local homeless shelters and food banks may accept donations of shark meat, or you can donate to the Share the Shark Foundation.

> NOTE: If your catch is a possible record fish, and you want to be eligible for a tournament or world record, do not gut or gill it before you weigh it. Mutilation of any sort will automatically disqualify your catch.

Before You Begin Butchering Your Catch

1. Bleed the Mako out when it's tied alongside the boat for a variety of reasons. If you bleed it out, you will have whiter, better-tasting meat. You could have a long travel time from the shark grounds to the port (such as only being able to travel at speeds of eight to ten knots because you have a shark tied alongside your boat). If you're forty miles out and traveling at ten knots, you would have a four-hour trip back -- a good amount of time to bleed out the fish.
2. After a long day of fishing, boating, and transporting the fish, it is usually late at night and you are exhausted when you arrive back at port. You probably won't have the strength to butcher the Mako that same day. Purchase at least $100 worth of ice and ice the fish down overnight.
3. Load the Mako into the bed of a pick-up truck and ice it down.
4. Bring the Mako to the scales, weigh it in and measure it. Be aware that sometimes the business that operates the official IGFA scales may be closed at the time you return to the dock.

5. Save a six inch piece of cartilage from behind the head for scientific research.
6. For the best-tasting meat, bleed and gut the Mako out at sea. If you want an accurate weight, be sure to weigh the organs out at sea or save them to weigh later.
7. Make sure you have the proper tools to butcher the Mako.

The list below details the brands I use for cutting the shark. However, you can use any brand as long as it meets the listed specifications. For more information on knives, see *Guns, Gaffs, and Related Equipment*.

- Industrial Diamond Eze-lap knife sharpener
- UPB-8 Combination Quickcut sharpening stone
- Sawzol blade
- High carbon-no stain 12 inch Mundial knife with poly handle, part no. 5617-12
- Forschner Victorinox 8 inch breaking knife with fibrox handle, part no. 40537
- Stanley FatMax drywall knife
- Large Ziploc heavy duty freezer bags with easy zippers

Optional Equipment
- Foodsaver Professional II home vacuum packaging system
- Plywood or table to use as cutting board

There are different ways a Mako can be butchered but I am going to list only one with photos.

Ideally, you want to have your shark hanging or alternatively you can simply lay it down.

Cut the dorsal fin off with eight-inch knife.

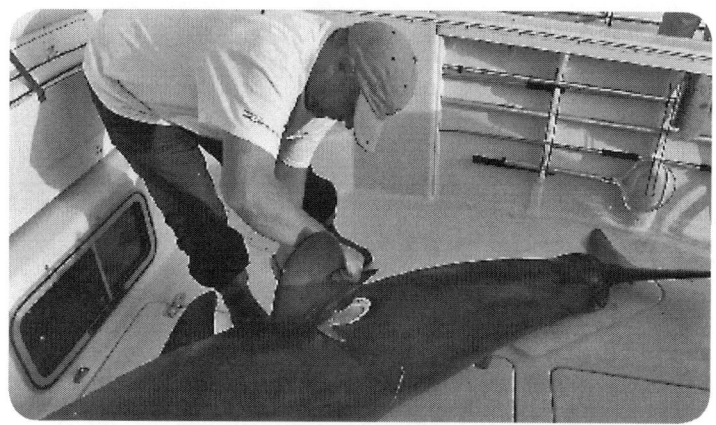

Cut the tail off above the keel with eight-inch knife.

Cut off the head with twelve-inch knife. If you want to save the jaws to mount later, be sure not to throw the head away. Be careful of the teeth, as they stick out and are very sharp. This is where most accidents happen while dealing with the head. You might want to freeze the head until you have a better time to cut out the jaws.

Roll the fish on its side and cut on the back side of the gills through to the peck fin.

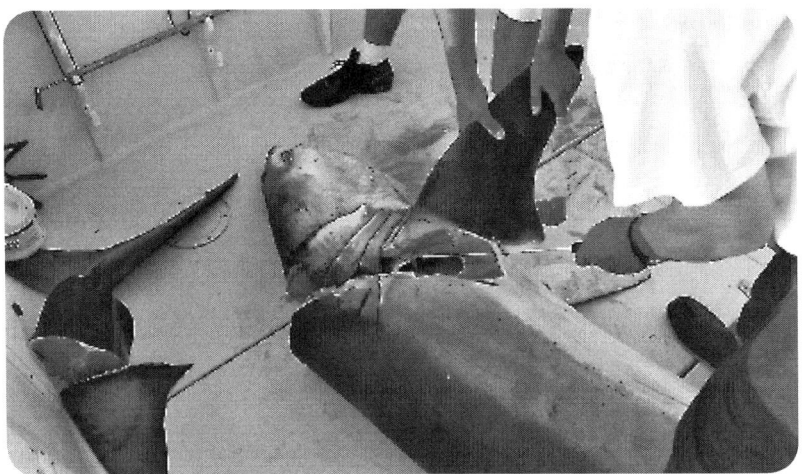

Cut through the skin starting from the anal area cutting all the way to the throat.

Roll the fish and cut behind the peck fin towards the head separating the peck fins and the head from the body.

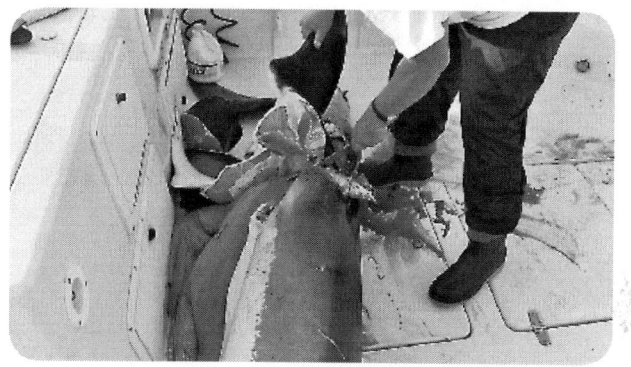

Cut the liver and gut from the head and move the head off to the side.

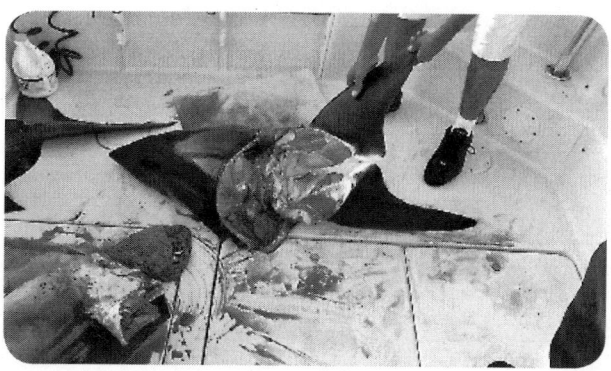

You might want to save the liver for chum,
for a future shark trip.

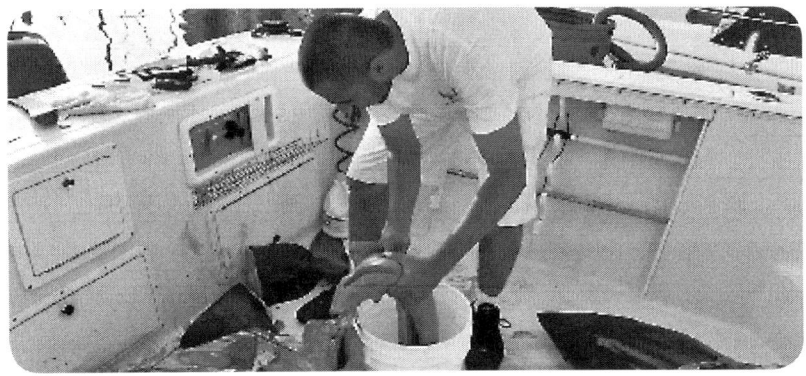

Roll the carcass as you cut it into sections approximately
a foot in length. Cut roasts with twelve-inch knife.

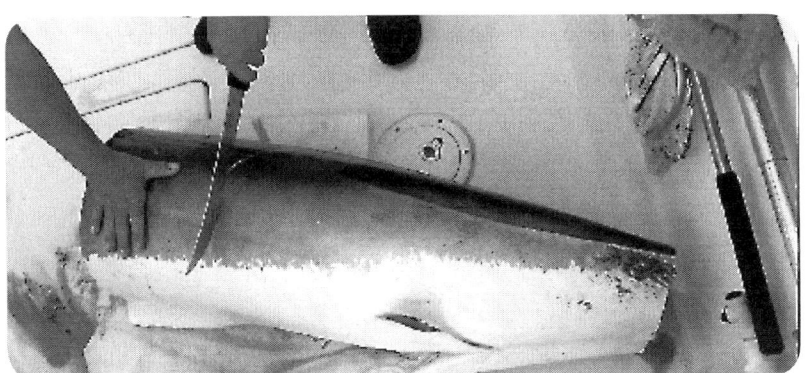

Once you have completed cutting all your sections,
proceed to cutting the steaks.

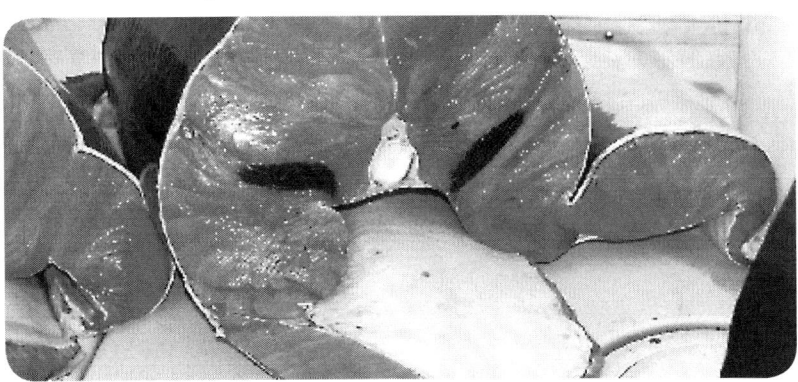

Cut the underbelly off (from pectoral fins to the anal fins) with a twelve-inch knife. The underbelly is white in skin color, so it should be very easy to distinguish.

Set the section so the skin is on the table and the meat is facing up. Cut straight down the edge of the cartilage to the skin, making sure not to cut through the skin.

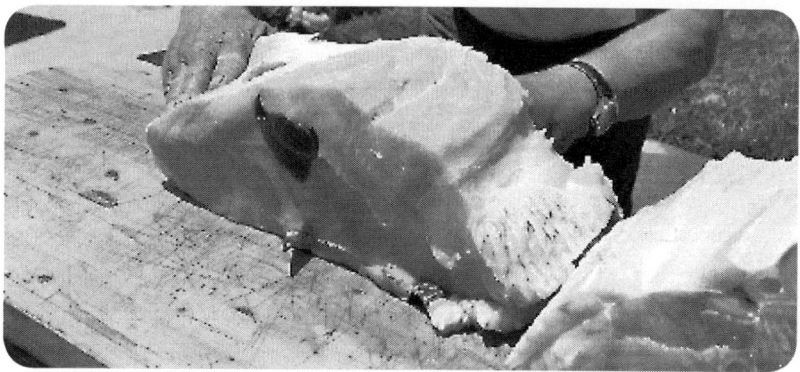

Cut from the center of the section on one side of the cartilage area down to the skin, across the skin, removing this section. Now turn it around and repeat for the other side.

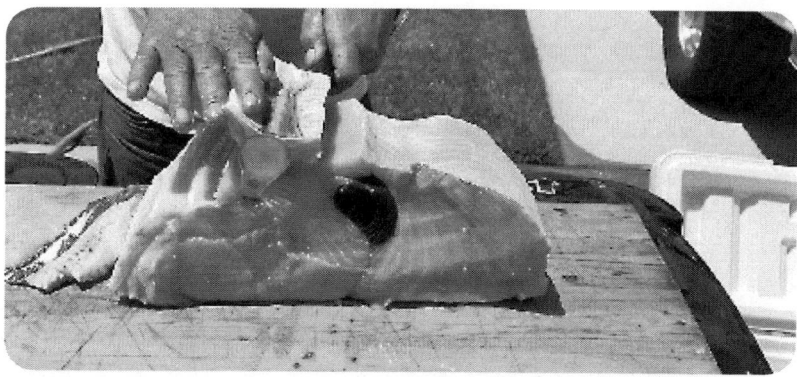

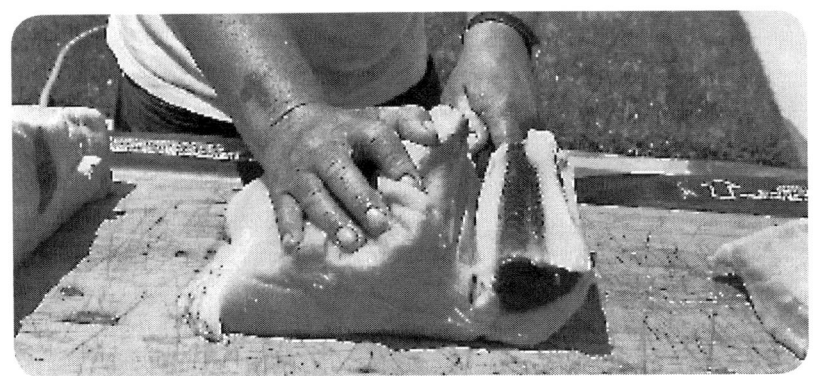

Now that the skin and cartilage have been removed, simply remove the blood line.

Cut one to one and one half-inch steaks. Keep the steaks on ice until they are ready to be bagged and put in the freezer.

COOKING THE SHARK

Whether you know it or not, odds are you have eaten shark meat before. I've seen Mako steaks sold as Swordfish. The skin is only way to tell the difference. The meat is similar in texture.

The best-tasting shark is a small shark. I prefer an 80 or 120 pound catch. I find them better tasting and easy to manage, when it comes to gutting, cleaning, and steaking it out. I usually keep one or two Makos a year for food, while tagging and releasing the rest. Remember that the large Makos are breeders.

The key to a good tasting shark is proper care of the meat. That means gutting and bleeding out the fish right away and cooling it properly, whether refrigerated or on ice.

In addition to being incredibly tasty, shark meat is very healthy as well. Almost cholesterol free and high in protein, it is nutritious and not fattening. A one-third pound serving of shark meat contains only 100 calories.

When cooking shark, let your imagination run free. Shark meat can be served in countless ways, including barbequed, broiled, fried, deep-fried, seared, or in a salad.

Bon appetite!

RECIPES

There are many ways of cooking shark meat. I will list a few of my favorite, simple recipes. For more recipes you will want to purchase a book geared specifically toward cooking fish.

Broiling or barbequing for shark steaks, tacos or salad

Preparation time: 30 to 60 minutes
Cooking time: 15 to 20 minutes at 400 degrees

- Ingredients
    - Shark steaks
    - Low-sodium teriyaki sauce
    - Lime juice
    - Fresh, minced garlic
    - Cooking spray
- Cooking
    - Marinate steaks for 30-60 minutes with teriyaki sauce and lime juice. If you do not have these or don't want to use them, you can substitute Italian dressing.
    - Place the steaks in a glass cooking dish. Sprinkle salt, pepper and garlic on the shark and cook in the oven for approximately 20 minutes depending on the size of the steaks.
    - Serve with your favorite side dishes and enjoy.

Shark Tacos and Shark Salad

- Ingredients for marinating the shark meat
  - Shark steaks
  - Butter
  - Lemon and pepper seasoned salt, garlic salt, or pepper.
  - Salad dressing or mayonnaise (optional)

- Ingredients for fish tacos
    - Shark meat
    - Corn taco shells
    - Cilantro
    - Taco sauce
    - Onions
    - Limes
    - Tomatoes

- Ingredients for Mako salad
    - Shark meat
    - Lettuce
    - Tomatoes
    - Salad dressing
    - Mushrooms
    - Baby corn
    - Garbanzo beans

- Cooking
    - Cook steaks over a grill, until evenly cooked throughout and golden brown (charbroiled). You want the steaks to be a little dry, as you will be adding taco sauce, lime juice, and salad dressing. Cook this longer than you would a well done steak, so it is not dripping fish juice.
    - Chop up on a cutting board into little squares. The pieces should be small enough to fit into the taco shells.

- If you are making tacos
    - Heat taco shells
    - Cut limes into slices
    - Serve with your favorite side dishes and enjoy.

Shark tacos make great party dishes. In my experience, people that normally would be turned off by the thought of eating shark have asked me if they could take some steaks home after trying a taco.

Shark Jaws

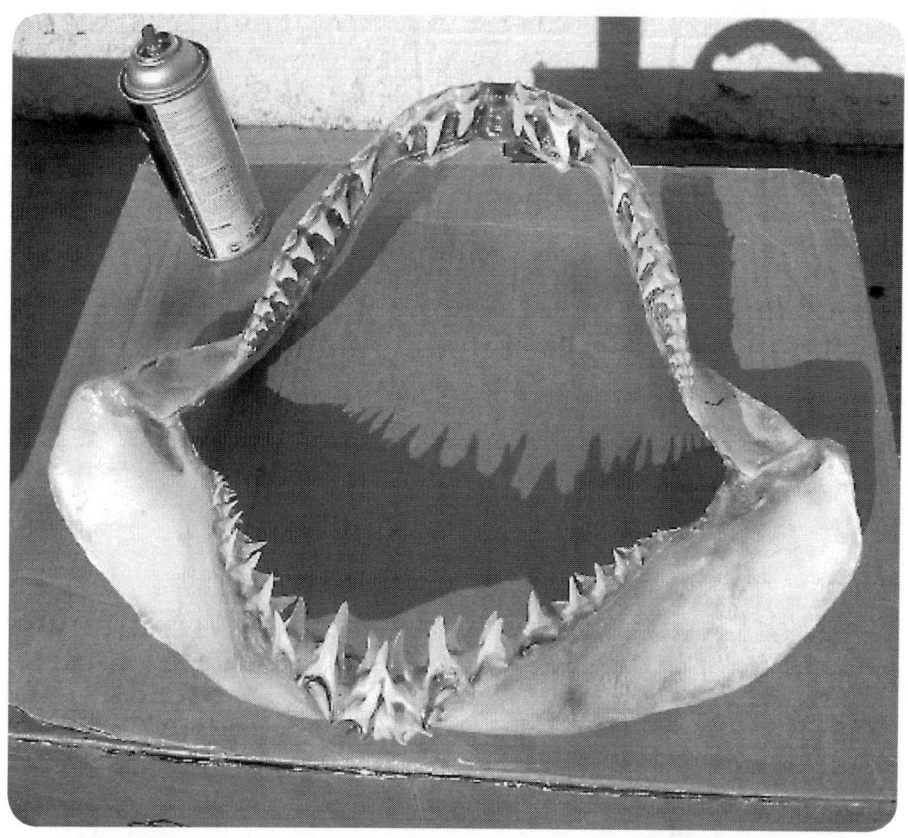

What better way to show off your catch than by mounting the jaws in your office or trophy room? Not only is it impressive to see a set of jaws hanging on your wall, but it is very attractive, and makes a great conversation piece.

While sharks are the Apex predators of the sea, it would be a waste to catch one solely for the purpose of making a trophy out of it. Remember, they are a very important part in our oceans ecosystem.

When you catch a shark, do not throw the head away. Even if you don't plan to make a trophy out of it in the immediate future, you never know when you will change your mind. By freezing it, you can always change your mind later or find someone else who would be interested in it.

> NOTE: Before you begin cutting the jaws, take warning. Just because the shark is dead, doesn't mean it can't hurt you. Even a closed-mouth shark extrudes razor sharp teeth. I remember one time while moving the head of a dead shark, I jammed my finger into one of the teeth that was sticking out. It pierced through my skin, stopping when it hit bone. Be careful!

Before you begin cutting the jaws, be sure to have the following tools and materials:
1. Gloves
2. Scraping knife
3. Fillet knife
4. Pliers
5. Knife sharpener/stone
6. Tablespoon
7. Five gallon bucket
8. Peroxide
9. Bleach
10 Wood strips for spreading the jaws

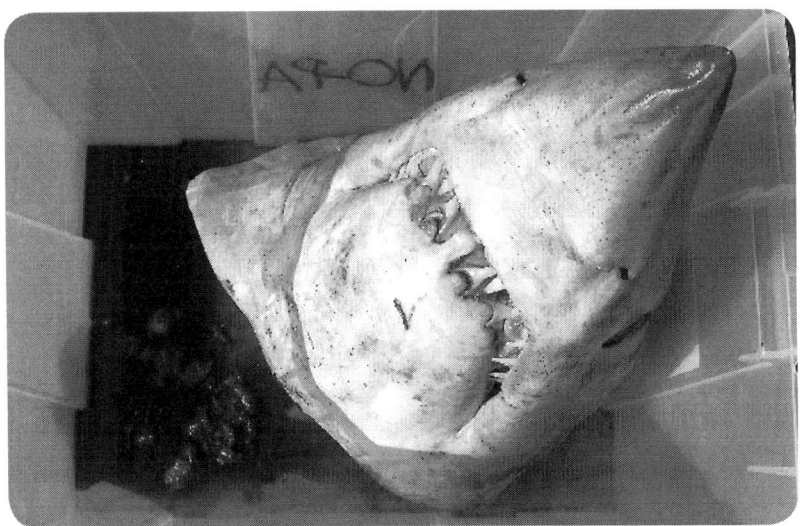

Remove shark head from the freezer and place upright into a tub or bucket to collect blood. Let thaw.

Set the head upright to minimize the amount of force needed when making your cuts, as you will be cutting in a downward motion. Pry the upper jaw away from the head with a sharp instrument, leaving the instrument in there.

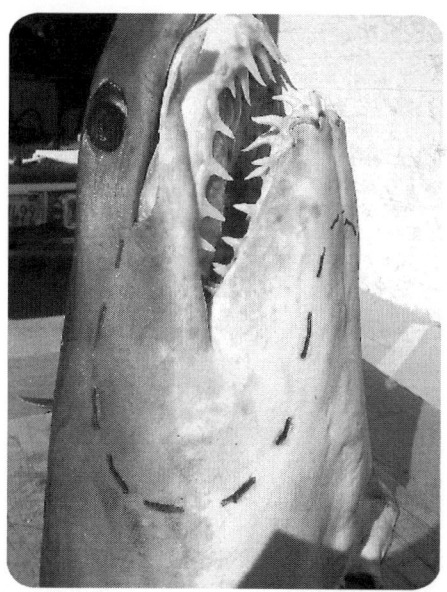

I added lines to the head around the jaw area in the picture above so you could see where to cut. If you've never done this before, adding lines to the head would be a good idea, so you can visually see where to cut.

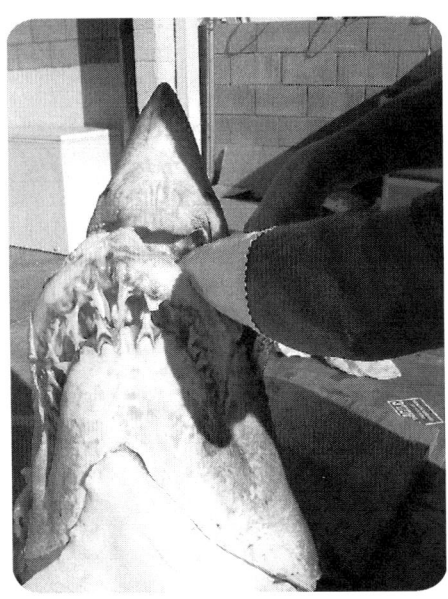

Begin cutting the upper jaw, going around the quadrant. Be careful not to cut the jaw cartilage. As you reach the lower jaw, you will need to cut the tongue tendons, to separate the tongue from the lower jaw. At this point the jaws should be removed from the head.

Discard the head. After discarding the head, cut and remove the throat area.

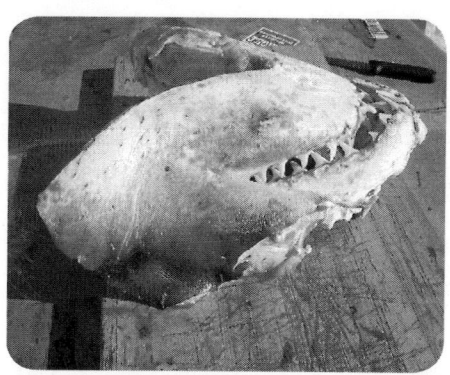

This is what you should have left.

Cut away all the skin right to the teeth, scraping off all the meat.

Now that the jaws have been removed from the head, clean as much meat off the jaws as possible. Use a fillet knife to remove the skin up to the teeth. Use a scraping knife to remove as much meat as possible. Use pliers to hold the skin while you make the cuts with scissors or a knife. Use a spoon to scrape meat off the cartilage.

Remove the gums from the lower and upper jaws to expose more shark teeth hidden under them. Doing this will make the jaws more impressive.

Once you've removed as much meat as possible, soak the shark jaws in 25% peroxide, 50% bleach, and 25% water solution for 10 to 25 minutes, constantly rotating the jaws. The jaws will appear bubbly because of the peroxide. Do not be alarmed. You just need to trust when it dries out everything will be fine. Just be careful not to overdo your soaking. Rinse the jaws with 100% water so the bleach will not yellow the jaws. I personally like a little yellowing to make the white teeth stand out more.

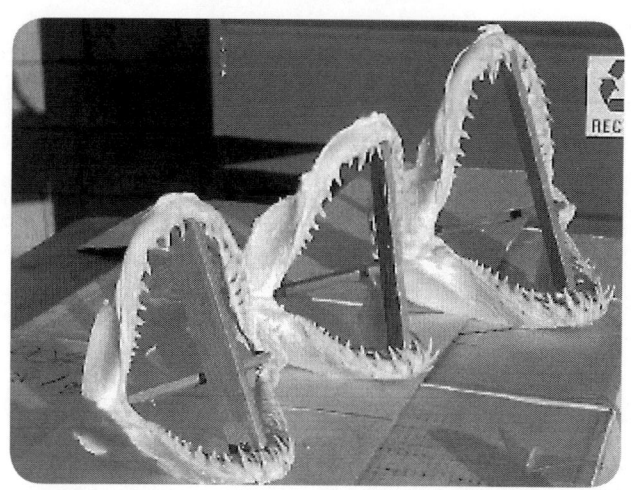

Cut wood strips and place them inside of the jaws with a snug fit, so that when the jaws dry out, they will retain the desired shape. Try to keep the shape as natural looking as possible. You must use two strips, one horizontally and one vertically. If you don't, when they start to dry the jaws will cave in. Do not use metal objects as they this will leave a stain mark. Let dry outside in the open air for a week or so.

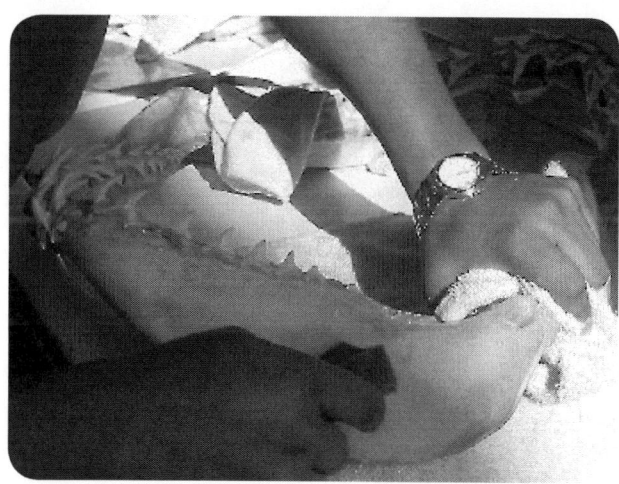

Once they've dried out, you may want to clean them up a little bit and sand them. I also like to spray a clear coat of varnish to give a nicer finish.

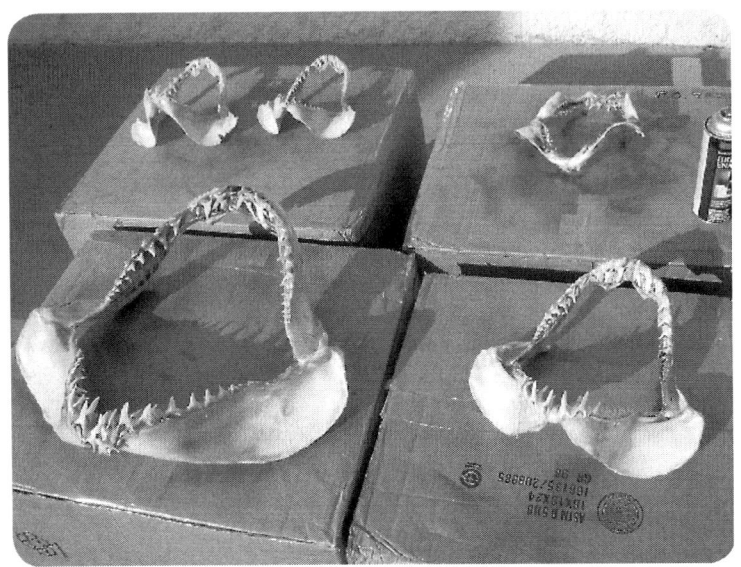

Completed shark jaws ready for wall mounting. Spray front and back with a clear lacquer paint. This will give the jaws a wet look and seal them up.

An easier way would be to call a taxidermist!

Shark Teeth

You can boil the jaws to remove the teeth and make jewelry. Once the teeth have dried, apply a coat of clear nail polish to the top of the tooth (to the tooth root area only). This will seal the tooth as the root area is porous.

I wrap the teeth with a gold filled 20 guage wire.

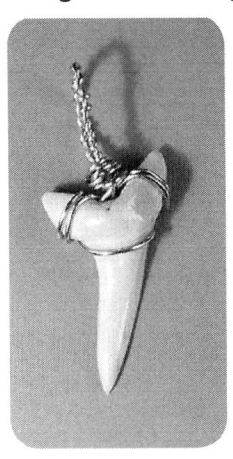

TOURNAMENTS

Shark Tournaments

Fishing in tournaments brings me a great deal of pleasure. Because of my team's hard work, I've had the privilege of placing (and winning) in several tournaments. I'm always proud to see their dedication and solid planning pay off.

There are many reasons to fish in tournaments. Tournaments provide a great way to meet new people and to make new contacts. Most fishermen are very outgoing and competitive by nature; entering tournaments provides an opportunity to show off your fishing skills, boat, equipment, and techniques. Tournaments allow you to prove that your team is the best on the water. Tournaments allow you to test the skills, techniques and drive of your team against other excellent teams. Also, businesses and corporations often sponsor tournaments to market their products; they donate boats and valuable equipment for prizes. Finally, the prize money (which is often substantial) is another great inspiration for fishing in tournaments. Most importantly, when sharks are brought to the scales at the tournaments they are studied by scientists.

Tournaments usually have two divisions, one which awards for the biggest catch and a catch and release division, which awards for the most catches. The catch and release division offers a completely different experience than catching a big fish, but one I find to be rewarding. Catch and release competitions offer a real opportunity to show of your tactics and skills. It's a great feeling to know that you can lure and capture more fish than any other team.

Sometimes people go to tournaments and get intimidated by the size of their opponents' boats. Don't let your opponents' equipment discourage you. Small boats win tournaments just as often as large boats. It's not the size of the dog in the fight, but the size of the fight in the dog that counts.

Costs

Fishing a tournament, while extremely entertaining and worthwhile, is costly. Costs can be as much as $3,500 with entry fees, daily side bets, hotel reservations, oil, fuel, chum, food, and other expenses. Splitting the costs with your teammates is very helpful. Despite the expense, I have always found the experience to be worth the cost.

Game Plan

Mental preparation begins when you make the decision to fish the tournament. You have to decide what qualities you need in your team, evaluate whether or not you have what it takes to make a winning team, and bring your team together. When you get your team together, you will be better able to determine if the team can be successful.

Picking the right teammates is very important. You are going to be with each other for at least a day or two (the standard length of a tournament), and if you and your teammates are not compatible, fishing the tournament probably won't be an enjoyable experience. Forming a weak team can put all of you into dangerous situations. Not only do your teammates have to be capable and compatible, they have to be right for their assigned jobs. As you organize a team you need to make sure you gather a group of people that collectively have the know-how, experience, and equipment to be able to conquer whatever challenge come their way.

After organizing a team, your next step (as the captain) is to prepare a team agreement and send it to each teammate. The itinerary should consist of 5 parts:

1. Date, time and location of the Captain's Meeting, a gathering traditionally hosted and led by the team's captain. The entire team needs to come to this meeting because each crew member's responsibility on the boat (who will be driving the boat, gaffing, chumming, etc.) will be finalized then.
2. Team roster and duty roster (who arranges hotel reservations, food, cameras, etc.)
3. Estimation of total costs to give the crew an idea of what they will be paying
4. Division of prize money and side bets
5. Sleeping arrangements
6. Rods, reels, hooks, bait, ice

Once your team is confirmed, you have several things to do. It is in your team's best interest to know what shipboard job each member prior to the tournament. Each team member also needs to be familiar and comfortable with the equipment he or she will be using.

Decide what equipment you will be using and which team member will supply each piece. Compare your team's rods and reels and try to put together a winning combination of gear. Your equipment needs will vary depending on your boat. For all the tournaments I've fished, I used 600 to 1000 pounds of chum, 43 gallons of water, 300 gallons of fuel, 10 gallons of oil, and food and drinks for my team for two days and one night.

Stock up on extra leaders and hooks. You should also bring maps, navigation books, a hand-held radio, an EPIRB, a million-candle power light, and cell phones. For safety, leave a float plan with your family or a friend.

Probably the most important part in succeeding in a tournament is finding the right place to fish (see Finding the Shark Grounds). I prefer to fish at high spots, current breaks, and deep canyons.

...e on a primary and some secondary fishing locations; this ...ecause your primary location may be crowded, or may not ... the results you expected.

Before you decide where you want to fish, you need to know ...at it is you want to fish. Are you looking for a monster Mako? Or are you trying to catch and release as many smaller Makos as you can? You can gain an advantage by scouting the waters a day or two before the tournament, and by talking to people who were recently out on the water.

Tournament Control

Tournament control usually consists of a minimum of two boats. They will document the hookup times, catches and releases, sizes, grid map locations, and GPS coordinates. Grid maps are maps provided by tournament control.

A grid map is basically a map with "grid" coordinates. An example of a grid coordinate would be Alpha, 7, corresponding to a location on a map with latitude and longitude locations. Any time you catch a fish and radio your catch to tournament control, you must supply your catch location according to the provided grid map. Try to match the maps you brought to the grid maps that are provided by tournament control, since grid maps usually don't include latitude and longitude or GPS coordinates.

Radio transmissions are the key connection for tournament control. When your boat is out of tournament control's range, you can relay information to tournament control via another boat. You may also need to provide this service for others. To prevent cheating and to allow tracking of each team's standings, tournament control must be notified any time you hook, catch, lose or release a shark.

Dealing with Cheaters

Like any other sport, shark fishing has its share of cheaters. Some disobey IGFA rules, like passing the rod to a mate or invading opponents' waters. You can do something about cheaters. This is one of the primary purposes for the existence of tournament control.

To report a cheater, either turn in a written complaint or call tournament control. If another team is fishing in your chum slick, radio their boat and point out the problem. If the team insists on fishing in your slick, talk to tournament control and they will get the other team to move.

Remember that tournaments are not geared toward professionals. Anyone with a commercial fishing license is usually unable to fish a tournament, as well as anyone who has been convicted of or is a known poacher. IGFA rules are strictly enforced at most tournaments, and it is smart to acquaint yourself with them. Using a spotter plane to help you find fish, getting assistance from another boat, and taking fish, gear, or people from another boat are all prohibited actions which will automatically disqualify your team. For IGFA rules go to www.igfa.org.

Qualifying Fish

Shark tournaments are much different today than they were in the past. In the past tournaments allowed almost all species of shark to count as placing fish. All kinds of sharks were caught during tournaments, but were discarded because they were not palatable. To qualify in today's tournaments, you must catch a Mako shark of a minimum size or weight. This way most fish caught during tournaments are released; only a few Makos are weighed in at the tournament's end.

Most all tournaments will have a requirement for qualifying fish. Traditionally, 58 inches (approximately 65 pounds) is the minimum. If a fish doesn't meet this requirement, you can still catch and release it for the catch and release division. You can measure a Mako with a tape measure. The consistency and accuracy level of the length to weight chart (which you should always keep handy; see page 180) is very high, and will suffice for tournament use.

If you are going to catch and release a fish, you have to take a picture of the fish with your hand and leader included in the picture. When you call tournament control, they will require you to take a picture of an object (which they will tell you) to show as proof that your picture is legitimate.

If you are far out to sea and have a fish to bring back (a potential winner), you need to calculate your speed, distance from the dock, and how long it will take to get back to the dock. You have to get to the scales before they close for the tournament, or the end of the day time determined by that tournament. Even if you don't think you are going to make it back, or that your fish isn't going to win, you should still do your best to reach the dock in time. One time while fishing a tournament I made it to the dock with only a few seconds before they closed the scales and was able to place in the tournament by making it in on time. Also you may find that your catch is now a winning fish because someone else got disqualified (because their fish was mutilated, they didn't make it to the dock in time, or some other infraction). Always think optimistically; no matter what, you have a chance.

The Big Payoff

The prize money is paid out of the entry fees paid in by each boat that enters a tournament. So the more boats that enter, the more money paid out. Side pot payouts are also based on the amount of money that is put in. If a team catches a large fish but did not put much money into the daily side pot they won't win much money. If you catch a smaller fish, but put more money into the side pots, you could end up receiving more money for your small catch than another team for their big catch.

Becoming a Winner

Here are some tips to help you become a winner in tournaments.

1. Since you've spent so much time preparing for a tournament (organizing a team, boat, and equipment), neglecting to prepare yourself mentally would be foolish. If you and your team go out on the water with the mentality that you are going to do the best you can and win the tournament, you're definitely going to increase your chances of winning, as opposed to just praying you get lucky and a monster swims your way. When fishing these tournaments, you should always play as if you are a winner. You never know what will happen in the end, and if you play as if every fish you catch is a winning fish; your odds at winning are much higher. Don't be disheartened because a fish looks small underwater; water can play tricks on you. If you see a fish and think to yourself, it's too small, I'm not going to go after it, you might let a tournament-winning fish swim by. One time I caught a skinny fish that taped out at 60 inches and the minimum weight for the tournament was 65 pounds, and to my surprise the fish weighed in at 70 pounds. Another time I caught one that taped out at 65 inches and weighed 105 pounds. Again I was surprised, because I didn't expect the fish to be any more than 80 pounds, yet it turned out to be a tournament winner.

2 Be careful to not let Blue Sharks eat your prize Mako and get your catch disqualified.

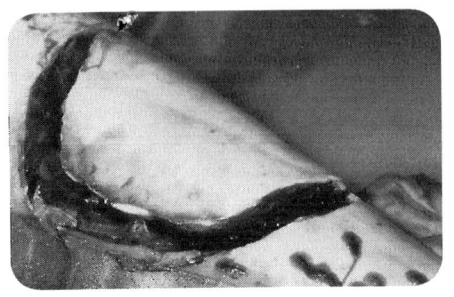 

Bites to Mako's from Blue Sharks

3. Misinformation is another important thing to consider. If someone radios in that they've hooked a 300-pound Mako, they may have given a poor estimate on the size of the fish, and it could be 200 pounds, or even the wrong type of fish! This happened in a tournament I fished. Someone radioed in they caught an eight-foot Mako shark, and then called back later to say it was a blue shark, not a Mako. Don't let anyone else intimidate you. As long as you play your best and find no excuse to give up, there's always a shot at winning.
4. During tournaments you probably won't be getting much sleep. It is important to not let your tiredness get the best of you. Always maintain good judgment, and just because you are tired you can't slack off or give up. One way to combat sleep deprivation is to designate rest shifts for you and your crew members.
5. A proven method for success is to go straight to a high spot to fish. Getting to a high spot first and claiming it for your team can have a huge effect on tournament success. If you can't make it to a high spot first, fish up the current from other boats along the high spot. This prevents other boats from fishing into your slick and gives you the flexibility of staying on the high spot and drifting onto their slick, of course keeping your distance. If other boats are fishing your chum line, ask them to move off. If they don't, relocate back up your chum line.
6. A problem I've encountered in Mako tournaments is having crew members go after Blue Sharks. When you are fishing a Mako tournament, only try to catch Makos. If you see a Blue Shark, leave it alone and sight fish. Catching a Blue Shark can prevent you from getting Makos, which is what you're after.

This beast was caught in a tournament.

Laws

Boating laws and regulations are there for a reason: your safety. If you don't care for your own safety, at least care for your passengers by obeying the guidelines and laws. This means to put the proper materials on your boat that will save their lives. Safety while fishing and physical stamina are needed to shark fish.

Fish per day
California state law/DFG says that you are allowed to keep two Makos per day, per angler, as of 2005. This law may or may not apply to other states, as state fishing laws and regulations may vary.

Inter-coastal Laws & Boundaries for private boaters
These laws apply to city, county, state, and federal regions.

> **SECTION 2. LIMITS OF THE TERRITORIAL SEA**
> *Article 3: Breadth of the territorial sea*
>
> Every State has the right to establish the breadth of its territorial sea up to a limit not exceeding 12 nautical miles, measured from baselines determined in accordance with this Convention
>
> **Source:** *http://www.un.org/Depts/los/index.htm*

International Laws & Boundaries for Private Boaters
Even now nations are disputing their maritime boundaries. Most nations are trying to determine these boundaries for economic reasons.

There are three types of Nautical Zone Lines. One is the Territorial Sea, two is the Contiguous Zone and three is the Economic Zone. U.N. tables show that 148 coastal nations claim a *territorial sea*, which is not supposed to include more than that ocean within 12 nautical miles (nm) of the coastline. About half of these nations also claim a *contiguous zone* which is up to 24 nm, also measured from the coastline. The contiguous zone allows states to "exercise control to prevent infringement of its customs, fiscal, immigration, or sanitary regulations within its territory or its territorial sea." Most nations also claim an *Exclusive Economic Zone* (EEZ), up to 200 nm, which consists of high seas within which "a coastal state may assert certain sovereign rights over natural resources."

Source: *http://www.un.org/Depts/los/index.htm*

Oceans and Law of the Sea

Firearm laws differ from county to county, and may or may not be applicable to international waters. The firearm laws are affected by inter-coastal and international boundaries. Also, find out where these boundaries are, and where they begin and end.

County laws may apply in *inter-coastal* waters, but do not in international waters.

You should check local laws regarding where you can and cannot chum. These may vary from county to county.

General Boating Rules and Regulations

Pick up a boating rules and regulations handbook from your local tackle or fishing shop.

DISCLAIMER: The information may or may not be 100% accurate, as regional laws vary. Please contact your local tackle store, library, or the internet for more information on laws and regulations.

A reminder, the United States Coast Guard has *ZERO Tolerance* when it comes to drugs, you could get your boat taken away permanently.

Shark Stories

SUBJECT: one word... MONSTER!

I've been fishing for sharks for years and have only seen two other sharks that would be in the same league as the won I caught last weekend. It could not have been caught at a better time!! With three cameras on the boat to document it!

I was contacted by the production company that was producing the first ever televised So. Cal. prime time shark tournament series (for OLN). They wanted me to get my shark fishing team together and do a day of tourney pre-fishing for the PCYC tourney. They were going to join me and film it.

Chum went in just before noon and the little Makos showed up right away. Of course the underwater cameras were there to capture it! A few hours passed... And the little guys kept coming in. I call them little because anything was little compared to what was about to appear.

What happened next will forever be imprinted in my brain. At around 5p.m. the seals split, the bait vanished, and the gulls left. I checked one of the chum buckets and it still had chum left in it, the other chum bucket was empty. I knew that the high tide was coming up and we needed to stick this out for as long as we could. I took some bait cut it up into chunks and put them into the bucket and placed it back in the water.

Bring the cameras along and look what happens, NOTHING! Then an image caught my eye. Was that a shadow? Cloud cover? Then I saw a swirl in the water that looked like twin Mercury 300 HP outboards taking off.

It was a Mako so big that when it finned its tail would FLOP FROM SIDE TO SIDE SLAPPING THE WATER!

I told the rod man to grab the rod, put it free spool, and get ready. I honestly felt like we were filming Jaws. The underwater cameras were in the water in a flash. The producer asks, "Is a big shark?" I smiled and said, "NO, that's a huge shark; maybe a White it's so big." I had to look at it several times before I knew it was a Monster Mako!

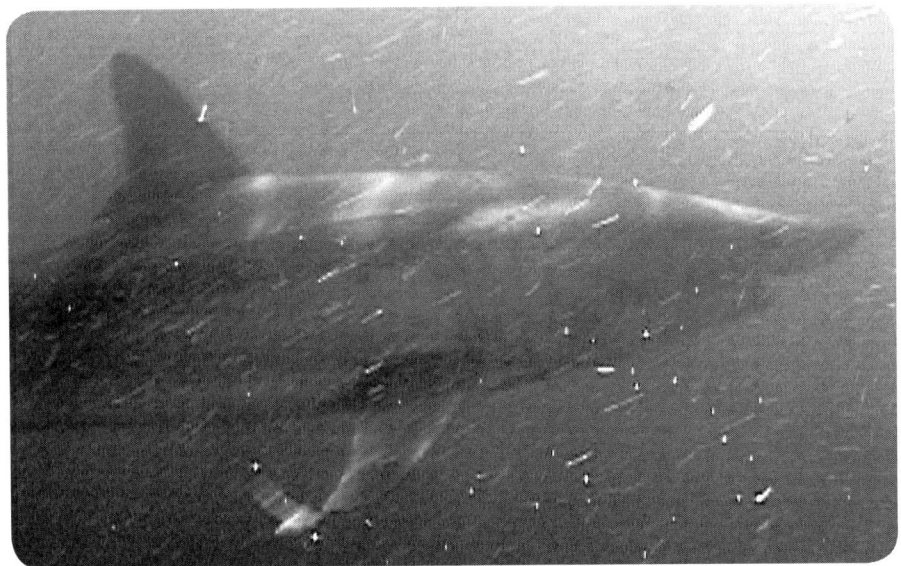

We filmed it for what seemed like an eternity as the monster swam round and round the boat. At times the shark was finning and on other passes she would go deep.

It truly was just like the movie, Jaws, as the shark would pass by the props and along the port side then across the bow. I literally stood right over her looking straight down, only mere feet under the surface. This was not a bus stop, but she was a bus! She looked more like a sub, a sub armed with teeth racked forward and ready to go!

The sight was so surreal that I did not even care to catch the beast, as watching her was so unbelievable!

It's funny how such an animal like this will make you go weak-kneed just by its sheer size. Scott asked me if I was going to fight the fish. I said, "No are you?" He said, "No". I told him, "That's why we brought the muscle. They will fight her, I am going to skipper the boat and you film her."

It was time to test the team out to see if we could muster what it takes to tangle with this giant prehistoric beast. I told the team that we were going to release this fish if we were successful in catching her. "Why release her?" they said. "Why?" I said, "Because if we were to subdue and kill the shark now before the tournament it would put the kybosh on us." Simply put, we would not have any success in the tournaments for another giant. Plus we had so much underwater footage that we needed to be thankful for that, and this fish needs to live to fight another day. "All agreed!" I said. "Yes" they said. "Let's do this!" I shouted.

We baited it and it ate. I counted out loud as the rod man looked at me and the then looked at his line screaming off the reel. I counted to seven and said, "Set it." He sets the hook and the shark goes NUTS!!! It then proceeds to jump three times next to the boat soaking the cameraman! At that moment I feared for my son's life as the last jump was coming back toward the boat. Then the line went slack, it spit the hook on the last jump. NO WAY!!! How did that happen? A once in a lifetime opportunity... GONE. Nope... 5 minutes later she showed up again. I have never seen a Mako shark do that, I could not believe my eyes. I frantically baited the hook and tossed it back out. I feared that this time she was going to take a little longer

to bite on the hook again. The shark made wide circles around the boat for a long time. Needless to say I was speechless and the rest of the crew were going crazy watching the fish swim around the boat. Some of the ideas being brought up on how to bait this fish were funny as hell. I stood my ground and told them to sit tight as I watched the sharks every move. The fish started to make tighter circles and I said, "Here we go, get ready she is hot now!" Sure enough, after a few real tight circles the fish went for the bait.
"HOOKUP"

The beast went NUTS again! She jumped several times and peeled line at a very high rate of speed.

I gave this beast the name 'Unknown' because the true weight of this beast will never be known hence, 'Unknown.' If I were to guess the weight, I would say not less 800 pounds and possibly up to or over 1000 pounds.

We chased her for awhile and were able to get her to leader several times. While at leader more underwater film was shot.

My seven year old son, Hunter, was into this drama the whole way through. Hunter had comments and suggestions like a captain, especially when we went in front of four tankers that were in a lined up row only a ¼ of a mile apart, while hooked up on

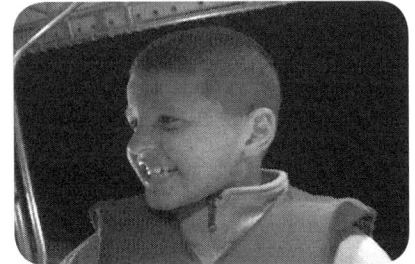

the shark with night falling upon us. Hunter was on tanker watch for awhile.

I told everyone it was time to cut the leader and let's do it before we lose all our light. Wouldn't you know it, after more then a half a dozen times of bringing that shark to leader for the camera she makes one more 300 yard run and goes deep. I was beside myself at this point, thinking, "If we blow  the release we'll lose her now." I did everything in my power to keep the situation under control. This fish was now going to bring us into the night for sure. With Hunter keeping our spirits high, we buckled down for the long haul.

For two more hours we fought this beast. Let me tell you that when I say it was pitch black out, it was black. It was one of nights where you can't see were the sky begins and the water ends.

I finally got her to come up from the deep to the surface. Once near the surface I said to the crew, "This is it. Let's not blow this. I want a clean release on film."

Scott got out the spotlight and I turned that beautiful Hotlines boat towards the fish. I set up the positions for everyone to take and we would play this out like pros. With cameras rolling we wired that beast over to the port side and I reached down and cut the wire. The shark drifted off silently into the dark. We watched in amazement and were yelling with joy. What a perfect day!

There are plenty of harrowing stories about sharks and shark fishing. Some stories you hear are fanciful tales that don't hold a grain of truth. Others are completely accurate and demonstrate both the excitement and dangers of the sport.

Just before we released the fish

Sometimes They Surprise You

The Fishermen & the 286.5 pound Mako

On May 23, 2001, at 10:15 a.m., John Mazur and I steered SEAWOLF (my Proline 2950) away from the dock. We were aimed on a heading to the 125 high spot just off the west end of Catalina Island. I intended to look around and check the area for sea life. My main destination was the 172 high spot. I had a Terrafin printout that showed a batch of warm water over the 172 high spot.

After passing over the 125 high spot we found no sea life in the 63.2 degree water. I was not impressed and plotted a course for the 172 high spot. One mile from the 172 high spot we came across birds, dolphins, bait balls, sea lions and warmer water (64.8 degrees). I knew this was the mother lode.

We set up and laid down a slick with whole bonito, blood and parts. We mashed them whole. I am convinced this is the right way to ring the dinner bell. Throughout the afternoon we tagged two Blue Sharks, lost tuna from our hooks to several small Makos, and enjoyed a trouble-free afternoon in the company of a bountiful sea lion population. Where was the sea monster we came to battle?

The end of the day was coming up fast. I opened the lid to the bait box and stared at the Yellow Fin Tuna that I had been cutting slabs off of for baiting the hooks.

"Are you thinking of using that whole tuna?" John asked.

"Well, yes," I replied. "It would take a really big shark to eat an entire Yellow Fin, and the little ones won't be able to rob us of this bait."

We bridled the tuna on a #12 hook and pitched it over. The smaller sharks nibbled at it several times. As the sun dipped toward the horizon, that end-of-the-day, worn-out feelings started to set in. It was about 7:30 p.m. so John and I decided to dump the chum barrel and call it a day.

As we were dumping the barrel, John yelled, "The rod!"

I looked back to see the tip of the rod doing the Mako dance. The balloon had separated from the line. Right then I knew we had hooked something big. Before I could look back to grab the rod the Mako was in an inverted back flip ten feet in the air between the balloon and the stern.

Luck was with us; the fish had come to the boat before he jumped and the line was slack. I quickly grabbed the rod, reeled down tight and set the hook. I passed the rod to John. The Mako took John around the boat twice, and then darted under the boat. I again took the rod and managed to get the fish out from under the boat and back to the stern. Suddenly the line went slack.

"Oh, no," I said, tired and deflated. I reeled until I saw the tuna head, then I put the rod into free spool and dropped the tuna head back into the water.

"Do you think he'll come back?" John asked skeptically.

"Not a chance," I sighed, "but what do we have to lose?"

The line started screaming off the reel. I couldn't believe it – the Mako had come back.

I told myself that this time the #12 hook would have to be set with brute force. I set the hook harder than I had ever set one before. I passed the rod back to John. The shark took him around the boat no less than ten times.

"Bring the fish to port," I yelled to John. "Next time he comes around I'll stick him with the fly gaff."

"I don't feel good about that plan," John responded. "The fly gaff is tied on the starboard side."

The sun was still giving us a little light on the port side. I had done this gaff maneuver twice before though both times it was not my first choice, either. We decided to give it a go. The chum barrel had been retied to the inside port cleat because the shark was attacking the bait when we emptied the chum barrel. There was no room left on the cleat for more ropes.

John brought the Mako in close enough for me to grab the 400 pound test wire leader. I pulled the Mako to the boat, reached the fly gaff under the shark and buried it in deep. The fish lit up, soaking both of us.

"Get on the other side of the rope!" I yelled at John who was still masterfully manipulating the dancing rod. "I can't hold him with only one fly gaff rope!"

John got pinned between the rope and the stern. He put the rod into free spool mode and set it down in the rod holder. Then he disentangled himself from the rope. He didn't seem really bothered by being trapped in the ropes, so I asked him to get another gaff for me.

I grabbed the second gaff and stuck the shark, but it was still not enough to subdue the raging beast. I grabbed another fly gaff and tied it off.

When I set the third fly gaff in the shark, the fight went out of him. At 9:00 p.m. the game was finally over. The Mako was weighed in at about 286.5 pounds the next day at the 76 fuel dock in Marina Del Ray.

The One That Should Have Gotten Away

I was lost in a sun-bleached slumber, when my buddy started screaming.

"Fin! Fin!" Adam shouted. "Get up, a fin!"

I sprang from my bunk.

"Where is it?"

He pointed toward the starboard side of the boat. I rubbed my eyes and took a hard look at the fin, which belonged to a Great White Shark. The Great White swam right off the stern of the boat through our chum slick and kept going. Later, a monster Thresher shark jumped out past the bait in our slick, but it was late afternoon before we encountered our intended quarry, a Mako shark.

Around 4:00 p.m., a tap, tap, tap on the tip of my fishing rod had me leaping across the deck for a good hold on the rod. I grabbed it and pointed the tip down toward the fish. Right then the line pealed off the reel so fast I had to apply a little drag pressure so that I would not get back lash. The fish leaped four times in the air, about 15 feet each jump. We ended up fighting it for one and a half hours.

My original intent was to release the fish. It was late in the afternoon and I really didn't want to have to haul that monster back to the docks. It was a 400 pound beast and towing it alongside the boat wasn't much of an option. It would have taken forever, considering we were so far out. Adam envisioned a different fate for the fish though. It was his first time to hook such a large creature and I guess his animal instinct told him to bring it home. I reluctantly agreed, knowing that having only two men to handle such a large fish was a huge mistake.

Nine foot Mako

After a long fight, I sunk a gaff into the fish and told Adam it was time to bring the fish inside the boat. Because of the size of this monster, I knew this wasn't going to be an easy task. I opened the swim step door, grabbed a couple gaffs and called Adam to help pull his catch in. While I was pulling on one of the gaff handles, I heard a popping sound and my right side exploded in pain. I had pulled my right arm completely out of the socket. After two years and extensive orthopedic surgery, I am still in pain every day. I wish I had listened to my gut instinct and released the fish instead of trying to get a 400 pound monster on board with only two people to haul it in. Besides you don't get your greatest reward from killing a fish. Just being out there on the water with these fabulous creatures and being able to fish are the real rewards.

A Great Fisherman, Lost

Billy Verbanas, a well-known charter boat captain who worked out of Delaware's Indian River Inlet, died while on a fishing trip in the Atlantic Ocean. He was stricken after trying to subdue a large Mako shark near Poorman's Canyon. Verbanas had the shark at the side of the boat while his crewmates attempted to wire it up. The shark shook its head and took a dive, taking Verbanas with it.

Verbanas was under water less than a minute, and his crew was at his side before another minute passed. Verbanas was waving his arms and seemed to be all right, so they threw him a life preserver. Verbanas stopped moving, so a man jumped in and pulled Verbanas to the boat. Verbanas was unconscious when they brought him aboard; his crew began CPR, radioed the Coast Guard and headed for the shore. They were pretty far out – it took almost an hour for a helicopter to reach the boat. A U.S. Coast Guard helicopter transported Verbanas to Peninsula Regional Memorial Hospital in Salisbury, Md., where he was pronounced dead on arrival, from injuries sustained in the heated battle with the shark.

The fishing community was stunned and saddened by Verbanas' death. Verbanas is remembered for two things – for helping people, and for catching monster Makos. Verbanas was a six-time Delaware state record-holder for Mako sharks; he landed a 925-pound Mako in 1990 and boated a 942-pounder in 1992.

Beware of Teeth

There are lots of sharp instruments onboard a fishing boat that can cause injury (gaffs, hooks, etc.) When you think about safety, remember to be careful with sharp objects. Shark teeth are also sharp objects and need to be handled with care before and after you catch a shark.

You always hear about careless people getting cut or bitten by sharks. In one tragic incident, a hooked Mako leaped into a boat with a seasoned fishing crew. While thrashing about on the deck, the Mako rammed one of the fishermen with its teeth, cutting a main artery in the man's thigh. He bled to death before anything could be done.

When there is a shark alongside the boat, keep the boat moving forward and the fish at a distance. That way the crew is safe if the fish jumps. Also make sure to know where the fish is hooked, and use a de-hooking tool to remove hooks. These tools make leaning over the side of the boat unnecessary, keeping you at a safe distance from the fish.

This Mako's teeth are snared up in the ropes.

Cockpit Time Bomb

It doesn't take long for the cockpit and deck to become a tangled mess. With ropes, gaffs, bait, and poles — not to mention rods, rod holders and leaders — lying all over the place, you can count on further chaos.

Imagine you and your crew have been careless and your cockpit and deck are completely disheveled. The leader man looks for his gloves and in the disorder, he can only find two left-handed gloves.

The skipper yells, "We have color on the fish!"

The leader man takes a wrap and pulls the fish to the boat. The gaff man steps in and makes a shot. A wire leader with a 12/0 hook has become entangled with a fly gaff rope which is now being pulled through the hands of the gaff man. So what do you do? Try to untangle the leader? Or tell the gaff man to let go of the rope?

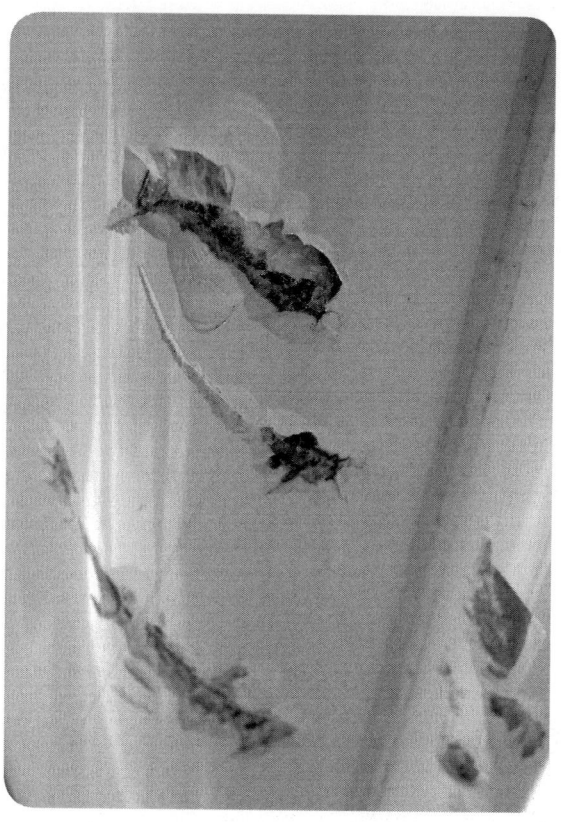

A Mako took a bite out of the cockpit

I've faced a scenario very similar to this one. The gear was cleared but no one noticed one of the wire rigs dangling overboard, hanging from a rod as the boat backed down on the fish. The boat charged down in reverse, and the end of the leader found its way into the prop, shutting down the motor. The accident could have been avoided if the leader was coiled up and put away.

Wire Hazards

It's not just a disorganized cockpit that's dangerous; the fish we chase and their brutish disposition makes them hazardous at close quarters. Most accidents happen with the fish at the boat and the leader in hand.

The most common leader accident is a crushed or broken hand. This can happen in a number of ways. For example, if the wire man has taken a couple of wraps of the wire leader the wrong way, it can cinch itself around his hand. The outcome is normally a broken hand or a swim with the fish. A pair of quality gloves which are a bit oversized are a great investment for anyone who plans on wiring a fish. You can remove them quickly and they will often come off by themselves when a large amount of pressure is applied to your hand. If you're fairly new to the sport or have no experience with wiring a big fish, don't take a wrap on the wire. Instead, save that for practice on a few small fish until you know how to dump the wire wraps.

One of the worst accidents I have seen came about when a crewman took the wire leader on a large tiger shark. He was having a hard time hanging on, and the shark lunged under the boat. The guy flew over the gunnel and was almost pulled over board.

On another trip, we were wiring to de-hook a blue shark. The rod was set in the rod holder as I wired the fish. As I pulled the wire in there was plenty of slack; the wire was hanging in the water. We pulled the fish alongside the boat, and were ready to use the release stick, when I bumped the rod it caused the wire leader to put three or four wraps around the end of the rod. At first I didn't think it was a big deal as our catch was only a 200 pound blue shark, but the shark went crazy at the boat and decided to take another run. I was certain I could hold the wire leader on this shark, but I overestimated my ability to manage 200 pounds of angry fish. I had to release the wire from my hands. I stepped back thinking the rod was an armed grenade about to splinter into a million pieces. Luckily, the wire slipped off the rod and stripped off the guides. I was thankful it didn't pull the whole rod and the $800 reel into the sea.

One minute I thought everything was under control, and the next minute all hell broke loose. That's part of the thrill of big game fishing -- you never know what's going to happen. The best way to stay out of trouble is to be aware of what can happen, keep your cockpit clean and uncluttered, and find a place for everything. Remember sharks are literally wild animals fighting for their lives.

Be Prepared for Accidents

Whenever you are shark fishing, remember that accidents can happen. You should always be prepared for the worst. Make sure you know where all your first aid equipment is, and be sure you are prepared to handle any situation that may arise. I've experienced many situations where preparedness was critical.

Once, on the first day of a tournament, I hooked into a very large Mako -- a tournament-winning fish. Each team member had an assigned job. While I was on the fish, Adam called Tournament Control, to notify of the hook up. Dan was driving the boat and John cleared the deck, prepared the gaffs, and was getting ready to wire the fish. John asked Adam to grab a pair of gloves from the helm access area and help him wire the fish. Adam got the gloves, and in his haste left the storage access door open.

I was fighting the fish. The boat was stopped and the fish was near the surface, off the stern. Dan came to the stern to see what was going on, leaving the helm unmanned. Tournament Control called to see what was going on. Adam took the call at the helm. Not realizing Dan had left the helm, I screamed for him to move the boat forward. When I looked at the helm Dan was not there; he was standing behind me and looking over my shoulder. Dan rushed to the helm to move the boat, yelling for Adam to get out of the way (the access to the helm area is only wide enough for one person). As the two passed each other in the access area, Adam severely cut up his leg on the hinge of the open access panel. Adam reached the stern and realized that he had cut his leg.

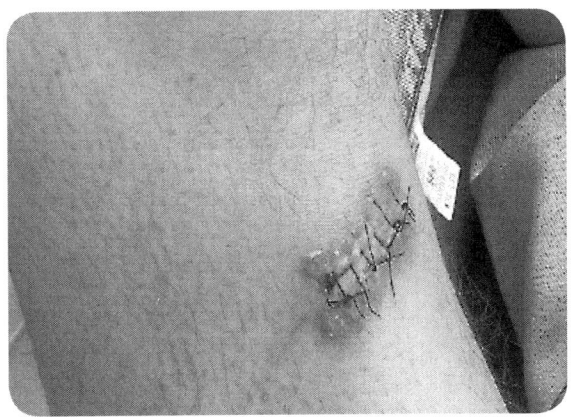

Adam, his bandage and our 194.5 pound Mako
3rd place tournament winning fish.

This put me in a quandary. As the captain of the boat, it is my responsibility to ensure the safety of the crew, but tournament regulations forbid whoever hooks the fish from passing the rod. The crew took care of Adam; they disinfected his leg and wrapped it up. The injury was serious and required stitches. We handled it masterfully because we knew the exact location of our medical supplies and had prepared ourselves to handle a serious injury. John sterilized the wound, stopped the bleeding and had Adam bandaged up within five minutes. Later that day, we took Adam to the hospital where he received stitches in his leg. We went on to place third in the tournament.

Obsession with the Sea

All season, my crew and I had been discussing filming a big shark being tagged and released, in an effort to boost the www.Sharks.us site. Summer was coming to a close and we hadn't accomplished our goal. We were feeling robbed. I realized that if we were going to go out and get this footage, we'd have to do it soon. Besides, it's at this part of the season that the big sharks bite.

It was the week of September 14th, and we were having a heat wave. Throughout the week, looking at the evening red sky, I knew it'd be a good time to go fishing. It had been several weeks since I'd been out on the water and I just had to go, no matter what, so I mentally prepared to go the coming Saturday. I had three things on my mind: getting the big shark footage, landing a world record fish, and (most important to me personally) just getting out on the water.

I knew that if I went out by myself my chances of getting good footage of a shark or landing a record were greatly diminished.

I made a couple phone calls during the week and couldn't find anyone to join me because of prior commitments. Still, I really wanted to get out there so I decided to go by myself. On Friday, I asked a couple of my co-workers if they wanted to come along. They both did and were committed to the trip. I was shocked. They were both incredibly excited that they were coming along. They had been exposed to shark fishing, but had never been out on the water. To make it easy on them and stress-free for myself, I told them to meet me on Saturday morning at their regular work time rather than embarking on an early morning venture. I prefer to fish for sharks in the late afternoon. I think that's when the bigger ones come out to feed.

We all arrived at the shop at eight in the morning, loaded the truck, and got down to the marina at nine. We loaded up the boat, went over to the fuel dock to gas up, I punched in the 172, checked my temp map one more time, and set a course. On the way out, I ran across a lot of life in the bay, consisting of bait, birds, sea lions, temp breaks, and warm waters. As we went further out we ran across a giant Mola Mola. I brought the guys over so they could take a good look at it. When they first spotted it, the fin was so far out in the water that they thought it was a shark. After looking at it for a bit, we moved along and scanned the horizon. I spotted a whale which they were excited to see. These guys got so excited and had so much fun. It was like they were on a wild African safari.

When I first arrived at the 172, there was a nice current break, lots of bait balls on the meter, and bait puddling on the surface, but another boat stopped on it at the same time. I did nothing for a while. A couple of other fishermen hailed me on the radio, but reported they had spent all night in the area for only a few blue sharks and runts. I was discouraged when I heard this, but then I thought about it for awhile. If they had chummed the area last night, where would it be now? I came to the realization that it must have been miles away by now, and so I felt reassured about sticking in my area. Besides, I really couldn't go out any further, seeing as how one of my guys was chumming his breakfast over the side. Twenty minutes had passed since I arrived. I took another look around the area and noticed that the other boat had left. I started the chum system and the motors, laying down a half mile slick. Then I turned the motors off and set the rods.

I climbed the tower to look for some sharks, and within a short period of time, a small blue swam into the slick. I wanted to get the guys hooked on something, so we baited and hooked it with the shotgun rig. One of the boys fought it, brought it in and released it.

As I was preparing to go back up the tower to spot again, it was hard to not get discouraged. We had one guy puking his brains out and the best thing we'd come up with was a three-foot Blue shark. Then, out of the corner of my eye, I caught a glimpse of a distinct, darting, Mako shadow off the stern of the boat. It looked small, maybe 50 to 80 pounds, so I grabbed the unbaited shotgun rig in my hand, looked some more, and saw nothing. Pulling a roughhouse move, I jumped up on the bait tank to peer down on the pee-green soup. I looked for a while and saw nothing, so I jumped down. A few minutes later, the Mako crashed on the balloon on the far rig.

I assumed the Mako had investigated both of the tunas and wasn't interested. I realized the Mako was actually larger than my first impression, so I grabbed the short rod and tried to make the tuna look alive. The shark darted across the slick, down deep, giving me a third look at it. I changed my estimate to 200 to 300 pounds.

I realized the shark wasn't interested in tuna, so I figured I'd bait it with the shotgun rig, and let the guys prepare for the fight of their lives. I pinned on a mackerel, threw it right where I saw the shark, and the shark immediately picked it up. I tried to get a quick hook set but ended up pulling the mackerel out of the shark's teeth. The mackerel was riddled with some really big teeth marks.

I immediately pinned on another mackerel and flipped it back, and once again the shark picked it up right away. This time the shark swam at the boat. I waited for the Mako to turn its head and swim away, and then I immediately set the hook. The shark took off as if nothing had even happened. As soon as it had taken some line out and applied some back pressure, it realized that it was hooked and started to scream the reel. I realized that this fish was going to have to be chased, so I had one of the guys get the motors going. We turned the boat around and begin chasing the fish. I went with one of the guys to the bow and decided to let the guys fight the fish. After I handed him the rod the fish took off on a long run. For some reason the inexperienced fisherman thought he needed to pull the lever back; the reel back lashed and we almost lost the fish. I was able to fix the problem and recover from it. Then I fought the fish to show the guys how to use the gear, since they had never done it before.

When I was done showing them how to fight the fish with the rod and reel, I handed back the rod, kind of like on-the-job training. For the first hour of chasing the fish into the sun, the three of us took turns with the rod. The fish made numerous runs, alternately submerging and riding along the surface. The fish's run was so spectacular. I was just waiting for it to go airborne so I could get some footage. The camera was rolling.

I asked the guys a couple times if they wanted to keep the fish or let it go. Neither of them really understood the concept of releasing, and so they said to catch it. I was also thinking about how nice it would be to stock the freezers for the rest of the year. At the same time I was thinking about how this would be the perfect opportunity to get some grade footage of a catch and release, so I wasn't exactly sure what to do. I really wanted to sink one of my new gaffs into something, and this was definitely a sizeable fish, but getting the video up for the www.Sharks.us website seemed to take precedence. I kept two fly gaffs readied in the stern, prepared for use in case I decided to catch it. Late into the third or fourth hour I made up my mind that I would rather catch some video than catch the Mako.

I made the decision to bring this fish to the boat, so I took over the helm, but was videotaping at the same time. I wish one of the other guys could have filmed, but none of them knew how to properly operate the camera. If I wanted footage, I had to take it upon myself. After about 45 minutes of trying to get some usable footage, I had to duct tape down the zoom button on the camera so my overeager assistants would stop adjusting it. I knew at this point I couldn't afford to risk any more poor footage, and I was very worried about getting the money shot on the release, so I didn't have much of a choice other than to film and navigate myself. I put one guy on the line and one taking stills.

I didn't want either of the guys to leader the fish, due to their lack of experience. I didn't want anyone to get hurt because they didn't know what they were doing. Of course with me being at the helm and filming, I couldn't do it myself. I yelled at the rod man to pump the rod as hard as he could, to get the fish to the boat. I overworked my rod man, the rod, and the gear trying to get some good footage. For a couple of minutes, I drove the boat alongside the shark getting footage, until it darted away. I needed to get the boat closer to the shark, and repeatedly yelled to the rod man to short pump the rod and bring the shark alongside the boat.

We repeated the process several times and each time the shark came to the boat it went down. It would have been really easy to just grab the leader and bring the shark in, but for the sake of getting video we did this instead.

Finally when the shark had had enough, we decided it was time to let it go. I left the camera hanging on my neck and grabbed the line to pull the shark toward the surface. The shark rolled over sideways to look at me, showing me its underbelly. I realized it was a monster! I knew that this fish had a bigger fight than the 515-pounder I'd caught recently, but I didn't imagine it would be as big as it was. This was the shark I wanted to get on film!

I knew that if I kept grabbing the line there would be trouble. I ran back to the helm, made an adjustment on the wheel, and outfitted myself and the sick guy with a set of gloves. We would try and lift the shark to the side of the boat for the money shot, which is a risky thing to do with a 700 pound shark. I was pretty convinced that if we could pull it to the boat, I could get some great footage.

In the haste of the whole situation, I didn't rationalize that it would be better for me to pull the shark and let the sick guy film. Both he and the rod man had had difficulty using the camera throughout the trip. What I didn't realize until later was that apart from the 45 minutes where the camera was zoomed in and out of focus, they had taken some beautiful footage.

One last time, I had the sick guy pull the line while the rod man stepped back out of the way. I kept one hand on the line and the other on the camera. The sick guy was see-sawing the line against the side of the boat. In his weak physical state he couldn't keep the line off the side of the boat, so the line rubbed alongside the boat and snapped, releasing our monster Mako back into the sea.

At the end of the day, we went home happy with our accomplishments. We got some great footage of a beautiful shark, and two guys who'd never been on the water before had the time of their lives.

A Monster by the Tail

One Saturday morning in August, the day of the Mako for Dollars Tournament, my boat was prepped with full tanks of fuel and about 500 pounds of tuna. My crew and I, along with our competitors, were hyped and ready to go at the shotgun start of the tournament. I checked out the areas we were going to hit on the Terrafin maps and started out for the 175. Luckily when we got out there, there were no other boats near us. As far as Makos, we didn't see anything near the boat all through the first day except one small pup. Then, just thirty minutes before time to stop fishing, a huge Mako came into our slick. It had to have been around 1200 pounds. The thing was the size of a bus. We took the bullet tunas off and put on giant albacore heads and whole tuna, but it just didn't want anything to do with what we had to throw at it. It kept coming up the slick towards the back of the boat, veering off to the port side, taking a look at us and then going deep. It did that repeatedly for an hour. We continued to fish even after the stop fishing time because this was a possible world's record. Eventually, we didn't see it anymore, so we called it quits and started back home.

On the way back we passed by a spot I call "Seal-Eater Island;" it looks like something out of *Jurassic Park*. This spot is a seal rookery. The seals go in and out of the island, but there is a death zone that they have to pass through where great whites hit them. The seals go through this zone very fast. I told my crew that we would head back to this spot the next day.

We re-supplied and met once again at 5:00 a.m. We decided to carry an extra 30 gallons of fuel; as it turned out, it was a good thing we had it. When we reached the island, we saw a nice break. Right after the break there were dolphins, seals, birds and bait as far as the eye could see. We had hit the mother lode! We went up a couple of miles and when the current break started getting colder, that's when we started our slick.

As good as the conditions were we really had nothing going on that day at all, other than dodging seals. At around 2:30 P.M., I was pulling bait away from a seal when the line started screaming off. I couldn't see the seal so I figured he picked it up and went running. The next thing I knew the seal went airborne, but the line was still pealing. Suddenly, right behind the seal a giant Mako shark went airborne. I think what had happened was the two met up at the bait and maybe spooked each other, but fortunately, the Mako had picked on the bait.

My eyes were as big as saucers when I saw this. It was a sight to see. When a thing of that size goes airborne it's like all time stops; you can't really grasp the magnitude of what you've just attached yourself to. I wasn't sure about the size of this Mako, but I knew it was fairly large.

Twenty minutes into the fight I was able to back down hard on this fish. There was water coming in over the back rail, but I quickly brought it to leader. In my book, twenty minutes is too early. If you bring a fish green into the boat, you don't know what's going to happen. I looked at that leader and I looked at my biggest crewman on board.

I said, "What do you think, you want to grab that?" He replied, "You just tell me what to do and I'll do what you say."

I thought about it for a second. I thought about my life and my crewman's life and then I realized that it's just not worth the few thousand dollars in tournament winnings. So we decided not to gaff the fish at that point.

We fought this shark for the next three hours. It took us several miles toward Santa Barbara Island and then turned around and went away from the island. We tried to lead it, but we could only back down on it. The fact that I couldn't plane or turn the shark made me think that we had a world record on the line, but it was getting late. I realized we weren't going to make the deadline for the weigh in, so we decided to just buckle down, continue the battle and see it all the way through.

We didn't know if we would become ineligible for a record if we switched up on the rod, but I needed a break so both of my crewmen took turns fighting the fish. After hours of fighting they became frustrated. I went back up on the fish and tried to fight it up for the third time, but all I did was lose line. It was horrific. At midnight, we considered cutting the line, but we stayed on it for another couple of hours until the shark started doing death circles, like a tuna. I knew we were close to the end.

It wasn't until 2:45 a.m. that we ended up cranking the reel that was now fastened to the rod holder and secured to another part of the boat. Slowly and carefully we pulled in the 300 or so feet of line until we got that fish to the boat. That's when we found out that she was hooked in the tail.

I yelled for John to get up and I quickly gaffed the fish. We secured this huge fish to the side of the boat as it made its last kick with its tail. Once the battle was over we tried to hurl the fish over the rail with no success. I even got out the wench and had no luck. Once I realized this fish was not coming over the rail, I punched up the harbor on the GPS and set a course.

With the fish tied to the side of the boat the max I could get out of the SEAWOLF was seven knots. Fully exhausted and beaten into submission I realized the trip to the harbor was going to take hours. Getting back to the harbor in the pitch black of night was going to be another fight in itself. Once we made it through the shipping lanes I turned the boat over to Jack. I couldn't stay awake for one more minute. Jack steered us home safely. We arrived to the scales just after sun up.

Even though we didn't win the tournament, the experience we had far surpasses any glory or money we could have won. It takes a lot of strength to pull something like that off, and it's not for the faint-hearted.

Appendix

Conversion Table (US to Metric, Metric to US)

1 fathom = 6 feet
1 mile = 880 fathoms

1 foot = 0.3048 meters
1 meter = 3.2808399 feet

1 yard = 0.9144 meters
1 meter = 1.0936133 yards

1 yard = 3 feet
1 foot = 0.333333333 yard

1 kilometer = 0.621371192 miles
1 mile = 1.609344 kilometers
1 mile = 5,280 feet
1 kilometer = 3, 280.8399 feet

1 kilogram = 2.20462262 pounds
1 pound = 0.45359237 kilograms

1 liter = 0.264172051 US gallons
1 US gallon = 3.7854118 liters

1 knot = 1 nautical mile per hour = 6076 feet per hour
1 mph =1 mile per hour = 5280 feet per hour

GPS Coordinates are based on time (hours, minutes, and seconds),
not distance (miles, feet, and inches)

Fork length is measured from the point of a fish's nose to the fork of its tail. Knowing the fork length can help you estimate the weight of a Mako.

Catches

Fork Length_____Total Length_____Girth_____lbs_____
M____F____ Water Temp_____Bait_____Line lbs Test_____
Date_____GPS LAT_____LON_____

Fork Length_____Total Length_____Girth_____lbs_____
M____F____ Water Temp_____Bait_____Line lbs Test_____
Date_____GPS LAT_____LON_____

Fork Length_____Total Length_____Girth_____lbs_____
M____F____ Water Temp_____Bait_____Line lbs Test_____
Date_____GPS LAT_____LON_____

Fork Length_____Total Length_____Girth_____lbs_____
M____F____ Water Temp_____Bait_____Line lbs Test_____
Date_____GPS LAT_____LON_____

Length to Weight Chart

U.S							
Total Length		Mass	Fork	Total Length		Mass	Fork Length
(feet)	(inch)	(lbs.)	(inch)	(feet)	(inch)	(lbs.)	(inch)
2' 4"	28	5	25	7' 4"	88	215	81
2' 6"	30	7	27	7' 7"	91	237	84
2' 9"	33	9	30	7' 10"	94	260	86
3'	36	12	33	8'	96	285	89
3" 3"	39	15	35	8' 3"	99	312	91
3' 5"	41	19	38	8' 6"	102	340	94
3' 8"	44	24	40	8' 9"	105	370	97
3' 11"	47	29	43	8' 11"	107	402	99
4' 2"	50	35	45	9' 2"	110	435	102
4' 4"	52	41	48	9' 5"	113	471	104
4' 7"	55	48	51	9' 8"	116	508	107
4' 10"	58	56	53	9' 11"	119	547	109
5' 1"	61	65	56	10' 1"	121	588	112
5' 3"	63	75	58	10' 4"	124	631	114
5' 6"	66	86	61	10' 7"	127	677	117
5' 9"	69	98	63	10'10"	130	724	120
6'	72	111	66	11'	132	774	122
6' 2"	74	125	68	11' 3"	135	826	125
6' 5"	77	141	71	11' 6"	138	881	127
6' 8"	80	157	74	11' 9"	141	938	130
6' 11"	83	175	76	11'11"	143	997	132
7' 1"	85	194	79	12' 2"	146	1059	135

Length to Weight Chart

	Metric				
Total Length (cm)	Mass (kg)	Fork Length (cm)	Total Length (cm)	Mass (kg)	Fork Length (cm)
70	2	63	224	97	206
77	3	70	231	107	213
84	4	76	238	118	219
91	6	83	245	129	226
98	7	89	252	141	232
105	9	96	259	154	239
112	11	102	266	168	245
119	13	109	273	182	252
126	16	115	280	197	258
133	19	122	287	213	265
140	22	128	294	230	271
147	26	135	301	248	278
154	30	141	308	267	284
161	34	148	315	286	291
168	39	154	322	307	297
175	45	161	329	329	304
182	50	167	336	351	310
189	57	174	343	375	317
196	64	180	350	399	323
203	71	187	357	425	330
210	79	193	364	452	336
217	88	200	371	480	343

An easier and more basic length to weight chart

Length-to-Weight Chart
Mako Shark

Fork Length (ft)	Min Weight (lbs)	Max Weight (lbs)
4	40	50
5	65	100
5.5	85	130
6	125	160
6.6	160	200
7	220	320
8	350	400
9	475	575
10	700	900
11	850	1,250
12	1,250	+

IGFA RECORDS for Mako Shark (as of 2006)

For a complete, up-to-date listing, please visit the IGFA website at http://www.igfa.org.

Men's Class
2 lb = 81 lbs, 9 ounces
4 lb = 165 lbs, 5 ounces
6 lb = 342 lbs, 0 ounces
8 lb = 278 lbs, 7 ounces
12 lb = 652 lbs, 8 ounces
16 lb = 699 lbs, 15 ounces
20 lb = 725 lbs, 5 ounces
30 lb = 977 lbs, 11 ounces
50 lb = 1080 lbs, 0 ounces
80 lb = 1075 lbs, 13 ounces
130 lb = 1221 lbs, 0 ounces

Women's Class
2 lb = 41 lbs, 14 ounces
4 lb = 37 lbs, 12 ounces
6 lb = 115 lbs, 0 ounce
8 lb = 107 lbs, 12 ounces
12 lb = 289 lbs, 3 ounces
16 lb = 331 lbs, 12 ounces
20 lb = 399 lbs, ounces
30 lb = 634 lbs, 14 ounces
50 lb = 679 lbs, 1 ounces
80 lb = 880 lbs, 0 ounces
130 lb = 911 lbs, 12 ounces

This is BIG GAME FISHING off So. Cal. There are 1500lbers lurking out there just off our coast. Some day the world record will broken, most likely from a Mako caught off of So. Cal.

ABOUT THE AUTHOR

Capt. Mike Schmidt has been fishing for sharks for more than a quarter of a century. His shark expertise is often called upon by researchers and media. He has placed in the Mako for Dollars, Pacific Coast Yacht Club, Mako My Night and the Mako Madness fishing tournaments, with several notable wins. He has won Mako Madness and Mako My Night tournament, in the most released fish division. His find and catch rate is very high and afforded several wins in that division. Schmidt served as Tournament Director for the 2003, 2004 and 2005 Mako for Dollars Tournament.

Capt. Mike Schmidt has done extensive work with juvenile great white sharks, placing satellite tags in the sharks and tracking them in the wild. Schmidt helped establish the Share the Shark Foundation, an organization dedicated to the distribution of shark meat to charities (including food banks and homeless shelters), allowing shark fishermen an avenue to contribute to their communities.

Capt. Mike Schmidt's articles and photos have appeared in magazines and internet publications across the continent. Schmidt produces the acclaimed shark fishing website, www.Sharks.us , which many tout as the world's #1 website for the sport.

For Schmidt the sport of shark fishing is about soul searching, the ocean's rejuvenating, positive energy, and becoming closer to God and His creations. Schmidt resides in California with his wife, Bari, and his three sons, Dillon, Hunter, and Conner.

Capt. Mike Schmidt is available for speaking presentations and other engagements. To schedule, please contact: 1-800-766-3425 or send an email to: Chum@Sharks.us

Made in the USA